OPPORTUNITIES

in

Biological Science Careers

REVISED EDITION

KATHLEEN BELIKOFF

VGM Career Books

Chicago   New York   San Francisco   Lisbon   London   Madrid   Mexico City
Milan   New Delhi   San Juan   Seoul   Singapore   Sydney   Toronto

The McGraw-Hill Companies

Library of Congress Cataloging-in-Publication Data

Belikoff, Kathleen.
  Opportunities in biological science careers / Kathleen M. Belikoff. — Rev. ed.
      p.   cm. (VGM opportunities series)
  Rev. ed. of : Opportunities in biological science careers / Charles A. Winter. © 1998
  ISBN 0-07-143187-X
      1. Biology—Vocational guidance.   I. Winter, Charles A., 1902–
  Opportunities in biological science careers.   II. Title.   III. Series.

  QH314.W525   2004
  570'.23—dc22   2003025821

    2 3 4 5 6 7 8 9 0   LBM/LBM   3 2 1 0 9 8 7 6 5 4

ISBN 0-07-143187-X

Interior design by Rattray Design

McGraw-Hill books are available at special quantity discounts to use as premiums and sales promotions, or for use in corporate training programs. For more information, please write to the Director of Special Sales, Professional Publishing, McGraw-Hill, Two Penn Plaza, New York, NY 10121-2298. Or contact your local bookstore.

This book is printed on acid-free paper.

OPPORTUNITIES

in

Biological Science Careers

To my sister Susan Martin Horn, whose love of science and
learning is the inspiration for this book.

And to my husband Larry A. Belikoff,
who makes all things possible.

Contents

and arboretums. Zoos and aquariums. Museums of
natural history. Volunteer service organizations.

General and systematic biology. Microbiology. Botany
and plant science specialties. Zoology. Entomology.
Marine (oceanography) and aquatic biology. Ecology
and wildlife biology. Genetics. Exobiology.

Physiology. Biophysics. Biochemistry. Pharmacology.
Nutrition. Immunology. Pathology. Clinical medicine.

Pharmaceuticals. Bioinformatics. Genomics.
Biomedical engineering. Agricultural sciences.
Forestry.

Educating children and nonscientists. Biocommunications. Technology transfer. Sales and
marketing. Law. Science policy and advocacy.
Regulatory affairs. Forensic biology. Biosciences
librarians and information service providers. Clinical
research.

Foreword

Is there anything more fascinating than the living organism? Ask any biologist that question and he or she will invariably agree that there is not. It's not hard to understand why biologists and other life scientists feel this way. These scientists possess an insatiable curiosity about plants, animals, and humans: they want to find out how living organisms are put together; what humans' reactions are to certain drugs, bacteria, or stimuli; how the environment affects a person's or animal's performance or behavior; why and under what conditions will certain organisms thrive while others do not; and so much more.

Perhaps you've asked yourself questions such as these. But even if you haven't, if these kinds of subjects intrigue you, a career in the biological sciences could be one that will absorb and delight you for many years to come. *Opportunities in Biological Science Careers* is a good place to begin to explore your interest. It will give you a broad overview of the many branches of the life sciences that are open to you, including botany, zoology, marine biology, ecology, genetics, pharmacology, immunology, and forestry, to name just a few. In addition, you will find practical advice on getting the right education, what kind of working conditions to expect, and how you will be compensated for the work you do.

It is fair to say that the areas mentioned above represent the more traditional aspects of the biological sciences. However, the author of *Opportunities in Biological Science Careers* also examines some related careers that someone with a bent toward this field may wish to consider. Biocommunications, the law, science policy and advocacy, library and information services, and sales and marketing are wonderful options for those who have an interest in applying skills such as writing, teaching, selling, or the law to a career in this field.

Whatever your inclination may be, a life's work in the biological sciences is one in which the rewards and level of personal satisfaction are great.

The Editors
VGM Career Books

1

WHY BECOME A BIOLOGIST?

HAVE YOU ALWAYS been curious about plants and animals? Did your high school biology class pique your interest in observing the natural world? Did you feel comfortable with the scientific process of laboratory experiments or field experiments? Or is it your overwhelming desire to make a difference in the world . . . discover a cure for cancer . . . save the environment?

If you answered yes to some of these questions, you should definitely explore a career in the biological sciences. With some research and self-examination, you can find a career that suits your individual interests and needs. As you investigate this career, you will discover that biologists—like other scientists—marvel at their good luck in getting paid for something that is so much fun. The motivation for following science as a career comes from within, and, for many, the urge to pursue science is as strong as a religious calling. Like a religious calling, the scientist's greatest reward is knowing that he or she has had a positive impact on humans and the other creatures of the earth.

Understanding the Science of Biology

According to *Webster's* dictionary, science is "the observation, identification, description, experimental investigation, and theoretical explanation of natural phenomenon." For many people, science is an exciting quest that challenges them to pursue the spirit of inquiry, the enthusiasm for exploration, the habit of rigorous analysis, the inquisitive outlook, the search for truth, and the willingness to discard pet notions once they are found to be mistaken. The scientist personifies our highest ideals of total objectivity and scrupulous integrity. As the biologist Konrad Lorenz put it, "It is a good morning's exercise to discard a pet hypothesis every day before breakfast: it helps to keep us young."

In the scientific world, there is an important distinction between pure science and technology or invention. The confusion is understandable. Science seeks to comprehend the forces of nature, and the scientist's reward is the joy of discovery and a contribution to knowledge. Technology, on the other hand, puts this knowledge to practical use. In some instances, the distinction becomes somewhat subtle. We sometimes hear about pure or basic research as distinguished from applied research, and there are arguments about whether scientifically trained people are truly scientists if they use their talents for making discoveries that they hope will lead to a practical result. Basic investigations often lead to practical results—sometimes years after the basic discovery has been made.

We are accustomed to frequent changes in our way of life brought about by new discoveries and inventions. This occurs often in the field of biotechnology. Some examples of the results of biotechnology include new drugs that help control diseases; new varieties of plants and animals that increase agricultural yields; alternative processing methods that bring us new foods (though not always improving on taste or nutritional value); and transportation speeds that can move us through the air faster than sound can travel. Such innovations often are regarded as advances of science, and many people believe that invention is the object of science. That is not really true, even though the inventions would not be possible without the scientific discoveries upon which they are based. Many very fine inventors are not scientists at all, and most scientists have never invented anything of practical value. For example, when the British biologist Alexander Fleming discovered that a substance produced by the bread mold *Penicillium* could kill bacteria, he was engaged in basic research, but in the end his inquiry led to the important practical result of the isolation of penicillin. This work ushered in a whole new era in medicine—the antibiotic era. However, penicillin would not have become a useful product without a large amount of practical research and the application of skilled technology. Hence, science and technology often work closely together, and enlightened industrial leaders have dedicated more and more funds to basic science. Today, much important ground-laying work in the life sciences as well as in other sciences is performed in the laboratories of industry.

Another distinguishing feature of scientists is that they don't have to pretend to know something in the field that they don't know. Scientists may guess what the answer will be and may have ideas about how to go about finding the answer; but if they don't know, it is not shameful to say so. A large scientific gathering was addressed by the then-president of the American Association of the Advancement of Science. Regarding a difference of opinion between himself and another eminent worker in the same field, he said, "Of one thing I am quite sure; neither of us knows anything about it." Louis B.

Flexner once said of his work, "Although I have confidence in the observations, I am far from wedded to the interpretations, which, in my opinion, badly need further work to test them."

How refreshing it would be if many people in other fields were to adopt a similar attitude! If you choose to become a scientist, you will be privileged to meet many people with such attributes, and you will be proud that you have chosen a career in science.

Biology is a group of sciences, rather than a single science. But no matter how the daily activities of one biologist may differ from those of another, all bioscientists are concerned one way or another with living creatures. All living things have certain properties in common, whether they are plants, animals, or microorganisms. All require sustenance derived from materials absorbed from the environment. They all grow and develop, and all respond in predictable ways to the environment. All of them depend upon reproduction to perpetuate their kind. All of these processes are governed by natural laws that are the same for all. Biology deals with all of these things—and more.

Many of the problems of modern civilization can be solved only by the application of biological knowledge. Examples of these problems are easy to find: pollution of air, water, or soil; the disposal of wastes; the effects of overpopulation and crowding; the use of drugs; the aging of the population; and the spread of AIDS (acquired immune deficiency syndrome). Improvement of the food supply and elimination of heritable diseases also are challenges to the biologist. Biology is involved in solving problems associated with descent into the depths of the sea and ascent to the highest mountains—and even into outer space.

You can readily appreciate that biology is much more than taking specimens of plants and animals into the laboratory and looking at them and describing what you see. It may interest you at this point to take a brief look at the types of biology and the range of careers available to those trained in bioscience.

The Many Branches of Biology

There is little consensus among the experts in the field of biology about what composes the subdivisions or branches of biology. To complicate matters, as scientists engage in more collaborative, multidisciplinary approaches to research, the lines between the sciences and their subdivisions become less distinct. Changes in technology also cause the creation of new branches of science. For the purposes of our career exploration we will be categorizing the branches of biology as "traditional"—those that have offered employment opportunities for many years and that may be familiar to you—and "nontraditional"—those that make up new job markets and may be unfamiliar.

One way to look at the traditional branches of biology is to consider that biology is the study of living things. If living things can be categorized as species (plants, animals, birds, and so forth), then the major branches of biology would be:

- Botany (the study of plants)
- Zoology (the study of animals)
- Ornithology (the study of birds)
- Ichthyology (the study of fishes)
- Herpetology (the study of amphibians and reptiles)
- Entomology (the study of insects)
- Mycology (the study of fungi)
- Microbiology (the study of microorganisms)
- Protozoology (the study of protozoa)
- Bacteriology (the study of bacteria)

However, some biologists choose to study various characteristics of all types of living things. Their chosen fields or branches of biology include the study of all or some aspect of all of the life forms listed above. Some of these traditional subdivisions of biology include:

- Morphology (the study of the shape and structure of plants and animals)
- Physiology (the study of the functions of cells, tissues, and organs of living things)
- Taxonomy (the classifications of living things into groups)
- Embryology (the study of the formation and development of the embryo in plants and animals)
- Genetics (the study of inheritance and variation in organisms)
- Ecology (the study of how organisms interact with their environment)

Collaboration among the sciences is not a new idea, although the concept of team research is more popular than ever. Some traditional examples of science hybrids that combine biology with other disciplines include:

- Biochemistry (the study of the chemical processes within organisms)
- Biophysics (the study of applying the principles of physics to living things)
- Molecular biology (the study of the chemical processes at the molecular level)

Other branches of biology are called applied sciences or technologies because research in these fields tends to focus on practical solutions to scientific problems. Some examples of these branches of biology include:

- Biotechnology (the study of biological applications that benefit mankind)
- Agriculture (the study of biological applications for food production)
- Forestry (the study of biological applications for lumbering and forest conservation)
- Wildlife biology (the study of applications that protect and conserve wild animals and native organisms)
- Pharmacology (the study of how drugs interact with living things)
- Bioengineering (the study of control mechanisms that regulate the actions of living things)

The nontraditional branches of biology tend to be newer disciplines that combine the science of biology with other fields in new and exciting ways. Some examples of these subdivisions include:

- Bioinformatics (the study of the application of information science or computers to biology)
- Genomics (the study of genomes—all of the DNA in cells including genes)
- Biometrics (the study of identification using biological characteristics)
- Bioeconomics (the study of applying economic principles to the biological sciences)
- Forensic biology (the study of living organisms in any context related to the law)
- Bioterrorism (the study of the use of living organisms to cause death or disease)

During a lifetime career, bioscientists may engage in teaching, research, administration, service work, or industrial production. Often, their chosen branch of biology changes because of special interests or an opportunity that better suits their needs or goals. As in any career, it is wise to be adaptable and be aware of changes in the job marketplace, while keeping an eye on your life goals. In a field as diverse as the biosciences, you are bound to find your niche.

The Continuing Evolution of the Biological Sciences

You have probably heard the expression, "There is nothing new in the world." This is certainly true of the biological sciences. Many recent discoveries are things that have existed forever; we just didn't know about them. If you examine the history of the biological sciences, you will see that people have been interested in uncovering the facts about the mysteries of life from ancient times until now. Even the newest of the branches of biology have roots in ancient times. Over the course of history, new names have been applied to bodies of knowledge that became recognized as a science, and new career opportunities were generated with each new discovery.

The Ancients

Like nearly everything else in our Western culture, biology can trace its origins to the ancient Greeks and Romans. In the fourth century B.C., Aristotle classified plants and animals, and his pupil Theophrastus wrote the first botany book. Some of the ancients' notions seem strange to us. Aristotle's theory that the same kinds of animals would be found on the same parallel of latitude around the world so misled Columbus that he was disappointed at not finding elephants in Haiti.

Biology Awakens After the Renaissance

The biological lore accumulated by the ancients was forgotten in Europe for more than a thousand years. Returning Crusaders brought back the ancient records kept alive by Arab and Jewish scholars in the Middle East. Even after the Renaissance, progress was very slow by modern standards. During the next three hundred years, only a few names stand out—Andreas Vesalius, the "father of anatomy"; William Harvey, who discovered the circulation of the blood; and Robert Hooke, who introduced the concept of cells as units of biological structure. In the 1600s, Anton van Leeuwenhoek devised the first microscope and discovered the existence of animals and bacteria too small to be seen with the unaided eye.

The eighteenth century witnessed several advances in what we would now call biochemistry. Joseph Priestley, an Englishman, discovered that green plants give off oxygen, while two Frenchmen, Antoine Lavoisier and Pierre Simon de Laplace, pointed out that respiration of animals is a form of combustion, like the burning of wood. The great Swedish naturalist Carl von Linne, commonly known by the Latin form of his name, Carolus Linnaeus, devised the scientific method of classifying and naming plants and animals that is in use to this day.

The Nineteenth Century—The Modern Age Arrives

The immense changes in our way of life that came during the nineteenth century also saw revolutionary new ideas in biology. Two Germans, Matthias Schleiden and Theodor Schwann, theorized that all living organisms are made up of cells. Another German, Justus von Liebig, discovered that plants synthesize organic compounds from carbon dioxide in the atmosphere and nitrogen from the soil. Louis Pasteur of France pioneered in microbiology and proved that living organisms do not arise spontaneously from nonliving matter—all life comes from life. His discoveries and those of the German bacteriologist Robert Koch paved the way for many advances in the treatment of disease, including aseptic surgery. An Austrian monk, Gregor Mendel, also discovered the principles of heredity during the nineteenth century, though his work lay forgotten until the beginning of the twentieth century.

No event in biological science in the nineteenth century had greater impact than the publication in 1859 of Charles Darwin's *The Origin of Species*, which set forth the theory that species of animals and plants gradually change over long periods of time because of natural selection. The idea that species could be transformed was not entirely new. Anaximander in the sixth century B.C. had proposed that one species could evolve into another. More than a century before Darwin's publication, the French naturalist Georges Louis Leclerc de Buffon asserted that species could change. Charles Darwin's grandfather, Erasmus Darwin, thought that species could be transformed by environmental influences. The Frenchman Jean Baptiste de Lamarck also had emphasized the fundamental unity of all life and the capacity of species to vary.

Even in the idea that natural selection brought about evolutionary changes, Darwin was not alone. Alfred Russel Wallace came to identical conclusions at the same time; indeed, the initial public disclosure of the theory was in a joint presentation of papers by Darwin and Wallace to the Linnaean Society in London. The subsequent publications in greater detail by Darwin, including *The Origin of Species* and *The Descent of Man*, have led to the association of his name, rather than Wallace's, with the evolution theory.

The Twentieth Century—and Beyond

In looking back on the developments of the twentieth century, we might call it the era of the popularization of science. Particularly after World War II, science came out of the laboratory and into people's homes, improving almost every aspect of their lives. The introduction of television brought glamour to science. Thanks to television, the first space walk changed our perceptions of life beyond our planet from fantasy to a reality that inspired generations of aspiring space scientists. To the television-watching public, scientists became heroes and explorers, not just the guys in white lab coats.

As children, many members of the baby-boom generation dreamed of joining Jacques Cousteau and the adventurous band of marine scientists on his ship, the *Calypso*. His undersea explorations were a source of wonder to many who watched his *National Geographic* television specials and read about his discoveries in magazines. Today, oceanography and the aquatic sciences are among the most popular career choices in the biological sciences.

In addition to television, the computer has revolutionized and popularized biology and the sciences. Microchip technology has been incorporated into all aspects of biological research, and access to the Internet has enhanced the opportunities for sharing scientific information. In fact, the management of the huge body of knowledge that constitutes biology today is known as the field of bioinformatics.

After World War II the demand for science-driven advances increased, as did educational opportunities, particularly for women. Ecology, one of the fastest-growing areas of biology attracted some of the most famous women in science. Many people credit Rachel Carson, a marine biologist by training, with the launching of the ecology movement. Carson's bestselling book *Silent Spring* is considered one of the most influential works of the twentieth century. Her indictment of the use of pesticides taught people to think about being connected to the earth in an interdependent way. Another conservationist, Jane Goodall, captured the hearts and minds of the public with her research on the behavior of the chimpanzees of the Gombe Game Reserve in Africa. Through her films, book, and *National Geographic* articles, Goodall helped millions of people understand the relationships among all creatures and inspired many to commit to preserving the delicate balance of the world's ecology. Today, concerns about conserving the Earth's resources influences nearly every branch of biology. In almost every field you will find references to ecology using new terminology such as "biodiversity," which is the vast array of living organisms—some yet to be discovered—in an environment, and "biocomplexity," the intricate interdependency of all living things. The conservation of our planet is so important that biologists are teaming up with other scientists to work on ecological solutions. This trend toward interdisciplinary teamwork in ecology is a model for how many bioscientists will work in the future.

Perhaps one of the most important developments in the history of biology occurred in 2003, when an international team of scientists completed the mapping of the human genome. The goal of the thirteen-year project was to sequence the three billion letters in the human genome, a task that was considered one of the most ambitious scientific endeavors in history. We now have an instruction book on the genetic makeup of humans, and this information will be the basis for detecting and curing many common diseases such as diabetes, heart disease, and mental illness.

The human genome project is a good example of how the history of biological research continues to build on its accomplishments. It is difficult to tell when research on genetics began. The selective breeding of domestic animals and food-producing plants can be traced to ancient times. In the mid-nineteenth century, Gregor Mendel, a mathematician-monk, conducted scientific research on the breeding of his garden peas. His observations became the basis of future research in heredity. In 1953 James Watson and Francis Crick won the Nobel Prize for describing the double-helix structure of DNA. Dr. Watson went on to become the first leader of the human genome project. As with most discoveries in the life sciences, progress is a double-edged sword. To its many critics, the human genome project was the key to a Pandora's box of ethical dilemmas. Cloning, using DNA to replicate a human being, is probably the most controversial future application of genomics. How far should scientists go in altering human life as it exists today? Are we playing God when we expect science to eliminate all of the abnormalities in Nature . . . and who gets to decide what is abnormal? Could you make those decisions? These are the ethical dilemmas that bioscientists face each day.

Profile of a Successful Biologist

The personal qualities that improve one's chances for success in biology are desirable in any scientist. This does not mean that all biologists have to fit a pattern or that all biologists are alike. Biology, probably the most varied of all the sciences, is broad enough to challenge anybody possessing curiosity about the nature of the world and of its life. As you read this section, compare yourself to the profile of a successful biologist.

Enthusiasm

The personal attribute that heads most lists of desirable traits for scientists is a genuine liking for the subject. Do you enjoy studying biology in high school or college? Do you like to read about science in magazines and newspapers? Do you find the performance of laboratory experiments an absorbing interest? If you can answer "yes" to most of these questions, you may possess one of the most important qualifications for success in a biological career.

Intelligence and Critical Thinking

Don't let the heading of this paragraph give you the wrong idea that only those of extraordinary intelligence can be good biologists. Emphatically, one does not have to be a genius to succeed in science; individuals such as Einstein and Pasteur are few and far between. People who can learn quickly can find a place in the life sciences. As in any field of endeavor, in addition to intelligence, imagination and creativity will help you get to the top of your chosen career.

Critical thinking, the ability to evaluate information and use it effectively to solve problems, is a valuable skill for any researcher. The process of scientific investigation involves sorting through many possibilities—which can often be conflicting and confusing—to find the valid result. Being able to deal with the often-frustrating uncertainty of research requires a mental toughness and intellectual discipline that transcends native intelligence.

Curiosity

Some years ago, the American Institute of Biological Sciences put it as follows: "This inquisitive outlook, this penetrating quest for the truth, is the most distinguishing characteristic of all biologists."

Advances in science have been made by those who wondered about things. This attribute is especially important for those who will enter biological research, but it surely is not out of place even in the performance of routine lab investigations or fieldwork. In addition, for the teacher of biology, the ability to foster an inquiring state of mind in one's pupils is a precious asset. If you wish to seek new frontiers of knowledge, there is no subject that will give you more satisfaction than biology. The quest for new knowledge takes biologists all over the world, from the icebound continent of Antarctica to the steaming Amazon rain forest, and from the tops of mountains to the floors of the deepest seas.

Open-Mindedness

A good biologist is willing to discard an old notion if it does not fit newly discovered facts. Occasionally, the discarded notion is a theory originally proposed by the researcher. Staying objective and flexible is often difficult, but essential, when a scientist is testing his or her own theories. A good biologist forms opinions not on the basis of preconceived notions, but on observed facts. This attitude extends to the environment as well. Keeping an open mind about working conditions, being adaptable in the role of scientist, and respecting the opinions of colleagues are also important characteristics of the successful bioscientist.

Precision and Organizational Skills

It will be useful to many biologists to be able to make observations with great accuracy and to detect minute differences between object and event. Two kinds of plants or two kinds of insects may look so much alike that the untrained observer would think they were the same; however, they may be of completely different species—that is, so different that they cannot interbreed. It may be equally important to recognize similarities. Small differences may be important in laboratory results. If you think that you cannot make such fine distinctions, it may be because you have never been called upon to do so; the ability to make accurate observations is a quality that can be learned, and every serious student of biology receives training in it.

For the scientist, precision is a skill that extends even beyond observation to the organization of practically all professional activities. Laboratory experiments and field studies are organized according to a set of principles called the *scientific method*, and this must be thoroughly understood and applied to the project by the lead scientist.

Patience and Persistence

When the great German biologist Paul Ehrlich sought to find a chemical compound that would destroy the parasite *Treponema* without killing the patient, he finally found it after trying 606 different substances. Although "606" has been long since superseded by better and safer remedies, its discovery was an important milestone in the history of biomedical science, for it initiated the era of chemotherapy—that is, the treatment of diseases with chemical compounds. Up to that time, the only agent that could be classified as chemotherapeutic was the ancient remedy quinine, which was extracted from the bark of the cinchona tree and used to kill malaria parasites. In that prechemotherapeutic age, Oliver Wendell Holmes, a physician as well as a poet, told the Massachusetts Medical Society: "If the whole *materia medica* as now used could be sunk to the bottom of the sea, it would be all the better for mankind—and all the worse for the fishes."

If Ehrlich and his assistants had lacked patience and persistence, they might have said, "We will try six hundred substances and if none of them works, we'll give up." This great advance, then, would have had to await the appearance of a more patient investigator.

Actually, Ehrlich was extraordinarily lucky, for most modern drugs are selected after trials of many thousands of substances. One of the modern antibiotics, terramycin, for example, was found only after the study of nearly one hundred thousand molds!

It is true not only in the field of drug therapy but in nearly all biology that most trails lead nowhere. One doesn't know that a trail is a blind alley until it has been explored, so one must follow a path for a while before starting all over again. Often the same manipulations and observations must be repeated over and over again with a minor modification each time until the true path is found. The general public does not necessarily appreciate that success is the exception rather than the rule, and that there is a great deal of trial and error associated with every great discovery. But most investigators take keen pleasure in the pursuit of knowledge and the joy of discovery—whether in the laboratory, the field, the classroom, or elsewhere—and this more than compensates for the long period of testing and measuring and repeating that goes on beforehand.

Other Personal Attributes

Probably the most important asset anyone in the workplace can have, including biologists, is the ability and willingness to work with others. People who can work with other people, especially difficult people, are usually very successful.

Successful biologists must be somewhat competitive. Whether it is vying for grant funding for research or climbing the academic ladder at a prestigious university or trying to get an article published in a peer-reviewed journal, biologists are not discouraged by rivalry. Like professional athletes who occasionally lose the game, successful biologists find opportunities for personal and professional growth in winning and in failure.

Writing, speaking, and the ability to listen to others are essential skills for the biologist. Biologists can obtain an enviable reputation only if their fellow scientists understand what they are doing, and this is communicated in the form of papers published in professional journals and in lectures at meetings and conventions. To a considerable degree, an aptitude for speaking and writing can be learned by study and practice, so you should not be discouraged if you think you lack this aptitude. For that matter, there are many very fine jobs in bioscience that do not require public speaking or writing, but generally these are not the top-grade jobs in teaching, research, or administration.

Certain physical capabilities are helpful in some types of jobs. For example, some of the duties of the wildlife biologist may require considerable physical stamina and strength, with some competence in outdoor craft. Arduous outdoor activity, sometimes in remote areas, may be required. On the other hand, there are laboratory and office jobs in wildlife biology, too. In some types of laboratory work, manual dexterity would be a valuable asset, particularly when one must manipulate very small objects. The degree to which this is required varies greatly among different types of biological jobs.

The chances are that if you are reading this book and if you have had some courses in high school science, you already have a fair idea as to whether biological science appeals to you. If it does, and if you are willing to work faithfully, you should be able to find immense joy and satisfaction and success in a biological career.

The Biologist's Conscience: Grappling with Bioethics

For the biologist, progress is a double-edged sword. With each advance there is both the potential to do good and the potential to do harm. In a society where the expectation for a high level of technology clashes with the limited availability of resources, the boundaries between good and harm often are blurred.

In addition to the personal attributes already described in this chapter, the biologist must have a strong sense of what is right and what is fair. This is what constitutes ethical behavior in the world of research. It is also the greatest intangible reward for choosing a career in the biological sciences . . . the knowledge that you leave the world a better place than you found it. But who gets to decide what is "better"?

Because the science of biology deals with the most precious of commodities—life—it is a discipline that is fraught with ethical dilemmas. We will now examine three types of ethical problems that face the biologist: eugenics, laboratory animal research, and integrity in the gathering and reporting of research data. This is a very superficial treatment of the gray area of scientific ethics. Fortunately, many high schools and colleges have incorporated the study of research ethics into their science curricula.

Eugenics

Every day there are stories in the news about how advances in biomedical research improve, and complicate, our lives. Perhaps one of the most controversial areas of biomedical research is genetics. The same science that improves the breeding of livestock and crops to feed the world's burgeoning population strikes fear in the hearts of those who remember the atrocities committed in Nazi Germany in the name of racial purity. Eugenics, the study of hereditary control by genetic control, is a relatively new term that describes the ancient practice of selective breeding and the new technology of genetic engineering.

Perhaps more than anyone else, biologists understand and respect diversity in nature. With the input of geneticists, the Canadian National Reproductive Technologies Commission recently proposed guidelines for new laws that would set limits for the use of eugenics in humans. These guidelines would outlaw activities involving the following: sex selection for nonmedical reasons; research involving genetic alteration of zygotes; prenatal diagnosis for susceptibility genes; and the attempt to enhance human traits. With enactment of this legislation, geneticists and citizens hope that new biological technologies will be used for the good of continued individual autonomy while maintaining the collective rights of society at large.

Laboratory Animal Research

Experimental research, especially in the biomedical sciences, has a certain glamorous appeal, and some discussions of careers in bioscience tend to equate science with experimentation. There are, however, other scientists who analyze and interpret an experiment that nature has performed. To presume that all biology is laboratory experimentation is as erroneous as the impression of some nineteenth-century philosophers that science is nothing more than observation and classification.

Those who perform biological experiments in the laboratory must of necessity make observations about living organisms. These organisms vary in complexity all the way from bacteria to human beings themselves. The elucidation of the functions of the human body has been made possible only by observations upon the bodies of animals most nearly resembling human beings, that is, mammals. Many people misunderstand animal experimentation, and you no doubt have heard the accusations of those who depict the experimental biologist as cruel and sadistic, inflicting unnecessary pain and suffering upon the victims. These people have had no experience in experimental laboratories. After forty years of experience in such laboratories and acquaintance with many hundreds of workers in them, I can only say that the cruel and sadistic experimenter must be a rare bird indeed—I have never met one.

Most experimenters know what their detractors fail to appreciate—namely, that observations made under conditions of extreme stress on the part of the animal subject cannot be considered to be made under normal conditions, and in most instances, the results might be invalid as answers to the questions under investigation. Experimental biologists have drafted a set of policies for humane treatment of animals in the laboratory, and a guide setting forth these policies has been assembled by the National Institutes of Health. It is a booklet entitled *Guide of the Care and Use of Laboratory Animals*, available for a small fee from the Superintendent of Documents, U.S. Government Printing Office, Washington, D.C. 20402.

Scientific Integrity

In his paper "Integrity in Scientific Research," Mark Frankel, former director of the American Association for the Advancement of Science, described the current crisis in the ethical behavior of some scientists: "Challenges to the quality and integrity of scientific research have become increasingly apparent in recent years with public revelations that some scientists have been guilty of fabricating data, falsifying results, and stealing the ideas and words of others." Although few would contend that such egregious conduct is widespread, most scientists acknowledge that it warrants a serious and effective response. However, while there is a consensus that fabrication, falsification, and plagiarism are clearly unacceptable behaviors, other types of conduct fall into a "gray area," where reasonable people may disagree over the proper course of action. These include practices related to selecting, sharing, and reporting data and research results; allocating credit; the role of mentors; publication practices; peer review; whistle-blower rights and responsibilities; and the treatment of intellectual property.

What contributes to questionable or unacceptable conduct of scientists? There is no single factor, but rather a complex set of intersecting influences that have combined to create a very stressful environment for researchers. The complexity of scientific problems and advances in technology have led to greater emphasis on large-scale collaborative research projects. It is not unusual for several laboratories, perhaps located in different countries, to collaborate on particular studies, but the sheer magnitude of such collaborative studies can make it more difficult to guard against sloppy work and easier for less scrupulous researchers to contribute fudged data to the project. The desire to strengthen the competitive position of the United States in world markets has encouraged universities and government laboratories to join forces with industry to produce innovations of commercial value. Such partnerships bring benefits to all parties as well as to the nation's economic position in world markets. Yet, commercial relationships may pose potential conflicts with some of the traditional values of science, such as openness and prompt publication. These changes in the complexity, size, and range of stakeholders that now characterize scientific research have placed demands on scientists that have outpaced the evolution of research norms and standards that researchers rely on as guideposts through rough ethical terrain.

To promote integrity in research, the U.S. Department of Health and Human Service, the National Science Foundation, and other government agencies and research institutions have established policies regarding ethical conduct in research and have developed procedures to monitor research projects and investigate allegations of misconduct. Other research organizations, such as the American Association for the Advancement of Science, have produced educational materials to prepare students to anticipate the ethical dilemmas they will face as research scientists and as responsible members of society who set the norms for acceptable moral behavior in science and in other facets of life.

2

Employment Outlook
for Biologists

According to the *Occupational Outlook Handbook*, published by the U.S. Department of Labor, the employment of biologists and medical scientists is expected to increase faster than the average for all occupations through the year 2010. The fields of biology that are expected to grow the most will be in genetic and biotechnical research, environmental protection, and biomedical research that deals with health issues such as AIDS, cancer, or genomics. Although there was very rapid growth in the biotech sector in the last part of the twentieth century, the number of new biotech firms is decreasing, and that will be reflected in a slowdown in hiring in the for-profit area. This is still the best bet for non-Ph.D. job seekers or for research scientists who want to leave the nonprofit research environment.

The Promising Employment Outlook

Historically, the number of new scientists joining the workforce has increased approximately 20 percent each decade, and this trend is expected to continue. Of the half million people in the United States today who call themselves scientists, roughly 150,000 are bioscientists. Of these about one-third are general biologists and two-thirds specialize in agriculture, forestry conservation, or the medical sciences.

Similar to many other professions, scientists in all disciplines are acquiring a more global perspective when considering employment opportunities. Cutbacks in both federal and private industry funding are expected to continue in the United States and Canada, while research expenditures are increasing in foreign countries such as Japan and Germany, where scientists are needed to provide the basic research that is the foundation for high-tech innovation. This opens many doors for scientists who have an interest in other cultures and countries and would enjoy pursuing a career while living abroad.

Competition for top jobs anywhere in the world will be keen in the twenty-first century. Job seekers with a doctoral degree in biology will continue to have the competitive edge for the best-paying positions. A combination Ph.D. and M.D. is becoming desirable for biomedical researchers who are qualified to follow their investigations from the laboratory bench to the clinical setting.

The employment outlook is expected to be positive for not only new entrants into the job market, but also for biologists currently working in the field. Because they are often involved in long-term research or grant projects, biological and medical scientists are less likely to be laid off than are other workers.

Tangible and Intangible Rewards

The rewards of a career in the biological sciences are both tangible and intangible. The tangible rewards include a safe, efficient working environment and a compensation package that includes a salary and benefits that will provide a comfortable living for you and your family. Perhaps even more important are the intangible rewards of this career choice. Throughout their careers, scientists experience continuous satisfaction and pride in knowing that they have had a positive impact not only on people's everyday lives, but on the future of our entire planet as well.

Part of the enjoyment of being a biologist is working in laboratories or classrooms or both, which are usually comfortable, clean, well-lighted, and adequately equipped. Many biologists choose more exotic work sites, such as an experimental field station or a research vessel. Most biologists will work in the company of others, and there will be stimulating interactions among fellow scientists, technicians, assistants, and others. For those few jobs involving the handling of hazardous materials, special training is available. Recent regulations from the Department of Occupational Safety and Health Administration (OSHA) require that all workers, including scientists, be well informed about the labeling, safe handling, and emergency spill procedures of any substance that can be toxic if opened or if there is prolonged exposure in the workplace.

Since competition for top scientists and technologists is keen, other features of the work environment or quality of life at work are often the deciding factors in choosing among employers. Biologists, like other corporate or educational professionals, are attracted to facilities that offer amenities such as access to personal and mainframe computers, on-site or nearby child care, exercise facilities, window offices and attractive surroundings, cafeteria or snack centers, a nonsmoking environment, access and accommodation for physically challenged workers, places and events that promote camaraderie among employees, and so forth. This environment, where casual dress (but not jeans) is usually considered suitable attire for under the lab coat or in front of the classroom, should be appealing to those who cannot envision themselves going to work each day in a suit and tie.

The other tangible rewards of a career in the biological sciences—pay and benefits—are meant to sustain the biologist's quality of life outside of the working environment. These rewards, often referred to as a compensation package, include:

- Salary, including bonuses and merit or cost-of-living raises
- Health, dental, prescription, and vision benefits
- Pension or portable (401k) retirement plans
- Profit-sharing, stock options, and tax-sheltered investments
- Direct-deposit banking and credit union
- Disability and life insurance
- Continuing education on-site for college degree and allowances for conferences
- Time off—vacation, holidays, and personal, sick, maternity, and other leaves of absence
- Working hours—flexible schedule, telecommuting, overtime pay, compensatory time off
- Transportation allowances—parking, train/bus pass reimbursement

Although comparing the salary figures offered by two or more employers is somewhat straightforward, analyzing the value of a cafeteria line of flexible benefits can be confusing. Employers are constantly redesigning their recruitment packages to gain the competitive edge in hiring the best candidates. That is why it is important to ask a potential employer for a written description of the salary and benefits being offered, and then carefully evaluate the entire compensation arrangement to see if it will match the personal and professional needs of you and your family.

The salaries for biologists vary greatly depending upon several variables. One of the most obvious is the type of employer you choose. Compensation in the for-profit, biotechnology companies, like pharmaceutical firms, is usually higher than salaries for grant-funded researchers working in a university setting. Other factors that affect one's paycheck are the level of education required, the scope of the job, the size and location of the employer, and the conditions of the labor marketplace. As in other professions, the law of supply and demand determines how an individual is paid. If your talents are in demand and there is only a small supply of other people besides you who can perform the job, then you are in the driver's seat for commanding the salary you want. If your talents are not in demand or there is a large supply of people including you who can perform the job, then the employer is in the driver's seat for salary negotiation. Many successful biologists learn early in their careers that keeping skills marketable is a survival tactic. Engaging in lifelong learning to add skills to your repertoire and staying informed about current changes in the biosciences marketplace are necessary to moving up the career ladder.

Fortunately, the marketplace for bioscientists is growing, and, therefore, the salaries are growing, too. The U.S. Department of Labor in the *Occupational Outlook Handbook* provides the following income information. For the most recent information, consult

its website at bls.gov. Starting salaries for college graduates with a
bachelor's degree averaged about $30,000, while master's-prepared
candidates started at about $35,000. The average salary for all biol-
ogists is about $50,000. The following are average salaries for other
biosciences positions:

General biologists (federal government)	$62,000
Microbiologists (federal government)	$68,000
Ecologists (federal government)	$62,000
Physiologists (federal government)	$79,000
Geneticists (federal government)	$73,000
Medical scientists	$58,000
Epidemiologists	$49,000
Secondary school teachers	$42,000
University professors:	
Instructors	$34,700
Assistant professors	$45,600
Associate professors	$55,300
Full professors	$76,200
Agriculture/food scientists	$52,000
Conservation scientists	$47,000
Foresters	$44,000
Biomedical engineers	$58,000
Clinical laboratory technicians	$41,000
Biology laboratory technicians	$33,000
Medical doctor	$160,000

In the federal government, salaries vary with level of education and
supervisory responsibilities. Salaries in private industry for similar
positions are about 10 percent higher.

Teachers and professors of biology are paid according to their level of education as well as the location and status of their institutions. Almost all college and university professors must have Ph.D.s and are paid based on their faculty rank.

Although practically everyone needs and appreciates a good paycheck, to the average biologist the deepest satisfaction about his or her career comes from things no amount of money can buy. For example, for the high school or college teacher of bioscience, the thrill of watching young people with keen minds react to the excitement of science cannot be described, only experienced.

Research work, administration, or any other kind of service in bioscience has intangible rewards no less than those of teaching. One of the most obvious things about life science is the enthusiasm most biologists have for their life's work. Not only is the work itself interesting, but most biologists take pretty seriously the idea that their efforts are worthwhile and that they can leave the world a little better than they found it. Perhaps this is one reason biologists are so much inclined to talk shop after hours, and maybe it explains why so many of them continue studying, thinking, and working after retirement.

Opportunities for Everyone

Recently biology, unlike some of the other sciences, has been successful in attracting a diversified pool of aspiring scientists. According to the U.S. Department of Education, women now comprise more than half of the biology graduates in the United States, and the number of African-American, Hispanic, and Native American students who major in biology has grown rapidly in the last decade.

This success can be attributed to the commitment of educational institutions, industry, and philanthropic organizations that have partnered to revolutionize biology education. In its recent landmark study, "Beyond Biology 101: The Transformation of Undergraduate Biology Education," the Howard Hughes Medical Institute reported on the "kaleidoscope of approaches" used by a number of colleges and universities to attract minority and nontraditional, especially older, students to the study of biology. The study cites the following rationale for the success of these programs:

> Innovative programs are demonstrating how to involve a broader cross section of young people in the sciences, especially women and minorities . . . the rapid growth of biological knowledge is itself a powerful force of change. Instructors know that they can no longer cover everything; instead, they are increasingly focusing on concepts that cut across scientific fields. Biology is building bridges to chemistry, physics, mathematics, information science, and other disciplines, requiring that its students become well grounded through the sciences. Classroom and laboratory instruction are emphasizing the flexibility that students need to master rapidly advancing specialties and techniques.

The sciences also have been at the forefront of offering opportunities to the physically challenged. There is little concrete data on the exact number of disabled scientists, probably because they and their employers are more interested in doing good science. In 1975 the American Association for the Advancement of Science (AAAS) initiated its Project on Science, Technology, and Disability. The project publishes a directory of more than one thousand scientists and engineers with disabilities who are willing to share their experience with others. The National Science Foundation provides Facilitation Awards for investigators, staff, and student research assistants who require special assistance or equipment to work on projects funded by the NSF.

3

WHERE WILL YOU WORK AND WHAT WILL YOU DO?

BEFORE WE EXPLORE the many varieties of career choices in the biological sciences, you might want to think about where you would like to work and what type of working conditions you favor.

Educational Institutions

Educational institutions that employ biologists include secondary schools, both public and private; colleges; universities; professional schools; and many kinds of technical schools. Teaching can be a most rewarding profession.

To make science education more interesting for both students and teachers, the curricula in high schools and universities has become more user friendly. The classroom and lab experiences are more integrated and emphasize problem solving and communication skills, not the acquisition of facts about biology. Teachers act

33

as mentors and old didactic teaching techniques have been replaced with interactive learning. Even printed lab manuals have been replaced with computer software that allows students to select tutorials that resemble sophisticated PC games.

The employment outlook for teachers trained in biology is reasonably bright. Many new teachers are required to replace those retiring or leaving the profession. Many states are attempting to increase the science requirements for graduation and are having difficulty recruiting enough qualified teachers to implement their plans.

The thirty thousand secondary schools in the United States constitute the largest market for teaching skills. The high school biology teacher is not charged with the responsibility of training professional biologists, but a good teacher will inspire some of the students to be interested in a biological career.

The teacher in secondary school, high school, or junior college will usually be required to obtain a good background of biology courses in addition to studying teaching methods and science education. Courses in chemistry and physics are also essential; indeed, in some small schools, a teacher may be called upon to teach more than one science. The college student who intends to teach biology should gain as much experience as possible in practice teaching. He or she also will find it advantageous to obtain summer employment in a biologically oriented job, such as work in medical or research laboratories, on conservation projects, or in forests.

Most biology teachers in elementary or secondary school have entered the profession immediately after completing college, but more and more find it desirable to obtain a master's degree. The standards for high school teachers are being elevated, and in some of the better school systems, a master's degree is the ticket for entrance. Training programs covering a five-year period and culminating in the master's degree are available in some training centers for teachers. Although generally needed for careers in teaching in a university, a Ph.D. or Sc.D. is not required for secondary school. This is just as well, for the emphasis on research that is necessary during the study for the doctorate is of limited value for the kind of work the high school teacher will be doing.

Not only is biology changing rapidly, but the methods of presenting biology to students have also undergone profound changes in recent years. The teacher must keep up with developments and is aided in doing so by organizations such as the American Association for the Advancement of Science, the American Institute of Biological Sciences, the National Science Teachers Association, and the National Association of Biology Teachers. These organizations publish periodicals and hold meetings that inform the teacher of new discoveries, as well as new ideas in teaching.

Unlike the secondary school teacher, the university teacher of biology is likely to consider herself or himself as primarily a professional biologist and only secondarily a teacher. College teachers usually earn a doctoral degree before becoming full-time faculty members, and doctoral training is strongly slanted toward stimulating interest in research. The advanced degree, Ph.D., or Sc.D., is awarded as a result of concentrated study of a highly specialized field, and colleges will consider hiring only those individuals whose specialized study is closely related to the subject that the new instructor is expected to teach.

The preparation for a teaching career in a college is the same as that for a full-time research worker. Most colleges and universities, especially the larger ones and those with the greatest prestige, expect faculty members to combine teaching and research careers. In that way, the college teacher not only passes along to the next genera-tion the knowledge accumulated in the past, but also keeps at the forefront of new developments. The young man or woman just beginning a teaching career in college may be given the title of instructor, but with some experience he or she can look forward to promotions—to assistant professor, then associate professor, and finally professor. With each increase in rank there is an increase in salary, greater opportunities to teach more advanced courses and guide young graduate students who will be the next generation of college teachers, and greater responsibilities in serving on commit-tees that help guide the policies of the institution.

Colleges offer many attractions for those considering a teaching career. They are frequently located in pleasant towns or in cities with many cultural advantages. The faculty members form a com-munity of people with a similar level of education and with many interests, hopes, and aspirations in common. To an extraordinary degree, the teacher is her or his own boss, and one is free to plan one's own time and to do the work in one's own way. Many uni-versities have several departments that employ biological scientists, while smaller colleges may have but a single department of biology. Colleges of agriculture, with their emphasis on applied biology, uti-lize an especially large variety of biological skills.

If you are considering teaching biology as a career, you should not overlook the possibilities offered by junior or community col-leges. Unlike the four-year college, the junior college often requires applicants for teaching jobs to obtain teaching certificates, but requirements for certification of junior college teachers differ from state to state. For specific information, contact your state depart-ment of education. The teaching load in junior colleges—the num-ber of hours per week actually spent in the classroom—is usually somewhat less than that required in high schools, but greater than that demanded in senior colleges. Often, salary scales are lower in junior colleges than in either high schools or four-year colleges, but in recent years, they have improved.

For more information, contact:

National Association of Biology Teachers
11250 Roger Bacon Drive, #19
Reston, VA 20190-5202
nabt.org
(800) 406-0775

National Science Teachers Association
1840 Wilson Boulevard
Arlington, VA 22201
nsta.org
(703) 243-7100

Governmental Agencies

The largest employer of biologists or of those whose work is closely related to biology is the federal government. Let us look, for example, at the Department of Interior, which is charged with the duty of conservation of natural resources. A list of the agencies within that department that employ bioscientists and biologically oriented people includes the Bureau of Land Management, National Park Service, Geological Survey, Bureau of Reclamation, Fish and Wildlife Service, and Bureau of Indian Affairs. The National Park Service has about a hundred natural areas where there are employees with a background in the life sciences. Amazingly, the large number of positions for bioscientists in the Department of Interior is exceeded by the Department of Agriculture, which is the largest employer of biologists. The multiplicity of jobs within the federal government is indicated by the following list—a very incomplete list—issued by various agencies and classified in biological sciences:

Agricultural bacteriology
Agricultural technology
Animal physiology
Bacteriology
Biological aide
Biology
Cereal technology
Cotton technology
Dairy husbandry
Ecology
Editor
Entomology
Fish culture
Fishery research biology
Forestry
Forestry research
Gardening
Genetics
Herbarium aide
Horticulture
Hydrology
Illustrator
Investigator
Librarian
Medical biology
   technology
Microanalysis
Microbiology
Mycology
Nematology
Nutritionist
Parasitology
Park naturalist
Park ranger
Pharmacology
Plant pathology
Plant physiology
Plant taxonomy
Poultry husbandry
Predator and rodent
   control
Range management and
   conservation
Seed technology
Soil science
Systematic zoology
Tree culture
Wildlife management
Wildlife research biology
Zoology

A career in government service has many attractive features for biologists. Employment conditions are good, and the increasing emphasis on life sciences bodes well for the future. The levels of jobs range all the way from blue-collar for those not yet fully trained, to the so-called supergrades for distinguished scientists. The websites of many government agencies contain career information and include a list of current openings and application procedures.

For those who start to work before completing their training, the government offers educational assistance programs. Arrangements are made for the employee to receive full pay while attending classes at a nearby university part-time, or even full-time up to one year. Of course, after completing this training, the employee is in line for a job with a higher rating.

Government positions offer a salary scale close to that found in private industry and somewhat better than that in the educational world. The government scientist has good laboratories and equipment and much freedom in doing the job her or his own way. The scientist in government can publish the results of the work in scientific journals and hence achieve a reputation in the world of science. Part or all of the expenses for attendance at scientific meetings also will be reimbursed. Other fringe benefits, such as group life insurance, health insurance, and retirement pay, are comparable to those available elsewhere. Although government service is centered on Washington, D.C., employees of agencies such as the Department of Agriculture, the Department of the Interior, the Public Health Service, and others are to be found in all the states; in some instances, their duties take them overseas.

All states and some cities employ biological scientists in roles similar to many of the federal jobs. Biologically oriented agencies of state and local governments include fish and game commissions, parks, aquariums, arboretums, and museums. Other jobs involve inspection or auditing of individuals and businesses to ensure compliance with regulations such as environmental concerns. Some local governments also run biological laboratories that perform crime-related research such as DNA matching or are involved in public health concerns such as monitoring for illness. On the average, these positions pay slightly less than comparable jobs in the federal service, and such fringe benefits as vacation time, sick leave, insurance, and retirement pay are not quite as generous as those enjoyed by federal workers.

For more information, contact:

USAJobs
U.S. Office of Personnel Management
1900 E Street NW
Washington, D.C. 20415-0001

Business and Industry

Industrial companies perform most of the research and development in our country. These companies have many jobs for people trained in the biosciences that are in nonresearch areas. For example, many industries depend upon microorganisms to help make their products. Some of these, such as cheeses, alcoholic beverages, and baked goods, have a long history, with records going back to about 6000 B.C. Others are of recent origin and owe their existence to new developments in biological science; prominent among these is the manufacture of pharmaceutical products by enzymatic action of microorganisms in large vats, followed by extraction and chemical isolation of the desired products. Some industrial biologists are using microorganisms for the production of methane and alcohol from waste products as alternate energy sources. Purification and recycling of water also gives employment to some biologists in industry.

Among those offering positions with biosciences training are processors of foods and beverages, manufacturers of cosmetics, agricultural industries needing the skills of those trained in animal or plant husbandry, breeders of fur-bearing animals, fisheries, forest products companies, and even concerns such as manufacturers of textiles, leather goods, and petroleum products as well as public utility companies and the aerospace industry. Still others are publishers of biological books, manufacturers of laboratory equipment, general laboratory supply houses, and those companies that make a business of collecting, culturing, and processing biological material for the use of educational institutions and research laboratories. There is scarcely any biological discipline mentioned in this book that is not represented in one or more of the industries just listed.

One growing industry is made up of companies that perform scientific services under contract for others. Some of them do biological testing or perform specialized research; others provide specialty services such as marketing, personnel, manufacturing, and consulting services. The customers of the biological testing companies include the U.S. government, drug companies, cosmetic manufacturers, and a variety of other individuals and corporations. Many of the customers have laboratories of their own but sometimes need the additional help or special expertise of a contract service company. The bioscientists who work for contractors are usually highly regarded as experts in their fields by their colleagues in other organizations. The biological disciplines represented in this industry include nutrition, biochemistry, physiology, pharmacology, microbiology, cytology, histology, toxicology, and pathology.

Manufacturers of pharmaceutical products probably employ more biologists than any other industry. The range of jobs in the drug industry includes biological manufacturing and packaging; quality control; biological testing of products; writing of brochures, reports, and correspondence; and training of workers. Especially noteworthy is the magnitude of the research efforts. More than twenty thousand people are employed in the research laboratories of this one industry, and an extraordinarily high percentage of them have a background in biological science. The demand for biologists and other scientists in the pharmaceutical industry continues to grow.

The research biologist in the drug industry is able, to a degree unmatched anywhere else, to work in collaboration with scientists in disciplines other than his or her own, whether it is in physical sciences or other biosciences. Cooperation between biologists and chemists is a daily occurrence, and the biologist often consults with physicists, mathematicians, psychologists, and pharmacists. Bioscience disciplines represented in the industry include physiology, biochemistry, toxicology, pharmacology, pathology, animal husbandry, microbiology, immunology, systematic botany, entomology, and nutrition.

The professional levels of biologists in the drug industry range all the way from beginners with baccalaureate degrees working as technicians to scientists of international renown. The beginner is encouraged to continue his or her education while receiving full pay from the company; most companies pay the tuition charges for part-time study at a nearby college or university. Many of the pharmaceutical laboratories are built in pleasant rural or suburban locations, in keeping with efforts to make working conditions as pleasant as possible. Salaries are slightly higher than in colleges, and the fringe benefits of vacations, sick leave, insurance, and pensions are among the most liberal of any industry.

Jobs with a biological orientation but outside of research departments are becoming more common in industry. Some companies prefer professionally trained representatives to present their products to customers. These are not salespeople in the old sense but individuals who provide a liaison between company and customer. Others employ professional people in training programs for sales personnel and technical representatives. If you can combine technical competence with a flair for writing, you will find that there is a brisk demand for staff writers and editors. In summary, despite obvious differences between academic life and industry, you will find the same types of people in both, and there are as many varieties of opportunities in one as in the other.

For more information, contact:

Biotechnology Industry Organization (BIO)
1625 K Street NW, Suite 1100
Washington, D.C. 20006-1604
bio.org

Self-Employment Opportunities

A growing sector of the bioscience marketplace is that of biologists who go into business for themselves. We have already discussed the biological testing industry; biological scientists started several of the laboratories in that category. Starting such a project requires an amount of capital that is not readily available to everyone. Easier to start are laboratories that perform testing services for physicians and hospitals. To be successful in such a venture, you should have a thorough background in the technical aspects of biochemistry, hematology, and the preparation of microscope slides. The more successful of such ventures have proven to be highly rewarding financially.

Self-employment opportunities are also available for botanists. Some of them become greenhouse operators who may engage in a particularly lucrative specialty, such as the growing of orchids. Botanical systematists become consultants to industry. Plant pathologists are also in demand as consultants, and some of them go into private practice. The number of self-employed botanists is small, but some find that their business pays well.

The collection, preservation, and sale of biological specimens is another source of self-employment. Vast numbers of living and preserved frogs, turtles, earthworms, sharks, sea urchins, anemones, seaweeds, seed-bearing plants, and other plant and animal organisms are used for teaching and research in schools, colleges, and research laboratories. The demand for them in the past has been met almost entirely by collecting wild specimens, but with the growing threat to the survival of many species, specialized farming must be considered as a source for the future. The demand fluctuates with the number of students of biology and the generosity of school budgets for materials.

For the senior scientist, independent consulting has become a lucrative occupation. Law firms are always looking for experts who can evaluate and corroborate evidence to strengthen their cases and, in fact, there is an entire field called forensic biology. The growing interest in the preservation of our natural resources has nurtured opportunities for consultants in almost every area of ecology. Biologists act as experts who prepare impact studies for new construction projects or can consult with lawyers who counsel industries whose work affects the environment. Consulting biologists also may be called up to draft legislation or serve on governmental or organizational committees that have been charged with developing policies dealing with concerns such as ethics.

For more information, contact:

Small Business Administration (SBA)
Local and regional offices are listed on its website: sba.gov.

Independent Research Laboratories

Research laboratories that are neither directly connected with industry nor a part of a specific department of a university receive their support in a variety of ways. Some of them depend largely upon the income from endowment funds that have been donated by an individual or group wishing to use its wealth in a constructive way. Others depend more upon annual contributions. Most of them accept grants of money from government funds or from interested industries. Whatever their sources of income, large numbers of bioscientists ranging in rank and status all the way from laboratory assistants to Nobel Prize–winning scientists find a stable and congenial atmosphere for their research. The same wide range of biological and biomedical disciplines is to be found in the independent research laboratories as in universities or industrial installations. The qualifications for appointment are the same, and salaries and fringe benefits do not differ greatly. In some of them, it is also possible to participate in the education and training of young scientists and to hold faculty rank in a nearby university.

There are independent laboratories in every section of the country. The following few examples will illustrate the wide variety of interests among these institutions, and you may note that some of them are so well known as to be almost household words.

- Jackson Laboratory, Bar Harbor, Maine, is famed for genetic studies, especially on unique strains of mice (jax.org).
- Marine Biological Laboratory, Woods Hole, Massachusetts, is a favorite spot for many biologists in the summertime, but it is active year-round in collecting and culturing marine organisms and in biological research (mbl.edu).
- Wistar Institute of Anatomy and Biology, Philadelphia, Pennsylvania, is not only a research and teaching center, but

also has been known as a source of laboratory animals, such as the famed "Wistar Rat" (wistar.upenn.edu).

- Mayo Clinic and Foundation, Rochester, Minnesota, is a hospital as well as a laboratory for a wide variety of research and training in the biomedical sciences (mayo.edu).
- Salk Institute of Biological Studies, San Diego, California, carries on advanced research on cancer and in immunology and other disciplines (salk.edu).
- Midwest Research Institute, Kansas City, Missouri, concentrates on general biological sciences, health sciences, and environmental science (mriresearch.org).
- Southern Research Institute, Birmingham, Alabama, engages in research in biology, chemistry, and various other sciences (sri.org).

Botanical Gardens and Arboretums

Botanical gardens typically have many varieties of plants growing in the open and more in greenhouses and conservatories. The care of these plants is much more demanding than that of the usual commercial greenhouse or nursery because a large botanical garden may have several thousand different species of plants, each with its own particular requirements for growth and propagation. In addition, botanical gardens and arboretums maintain collections of dried specimens. These collections can be very large—the New York Botanical Garden has more than three million specimens. Botanical gardens are also educational institutions, and many of them conduct extensive research. Some of the subjects of research are ecology, plant anatomy, systematic botany, economic botany, plant physiology, phytopathology, and biochemistry. Sometimes research botanists and curators hold professorships in nearby universities. Graduate students in some departments of botany can complete all their research for advanced degrees at a botanical garden or arboretum.

Botanical gardens offer educational programs to schoolchildren and to the general public. These programs consist not only of labeled collections of plants, but also of exhibits, classes, lectures, publications, and the furnishing of background material in botany for schools at all levels. Staff members especially skilled in these activities have not always been easy to find, and directors of the gardens are on the lookout for promising candidates.

The kinds of jobs available in botanical gardens and arboretums include gardeners, horticulturists, caretakers for the herbarium, staff members for preparing exhibits, directors of educational activities, editors and writers for the publication programs, librarians, and research scientists. If you wish to consider a career in this field, you should visit at least one botanical garden or arboretum, and preferably more than one, since they differ markedly in size, organization, and activities. Make an appointment with the director or other staff member, discuss your interests with him or her, and observe the place in action.

For more information, contact:

American Association of Botanic Gardens and Arboreta
100 West Tenth Street, Suite 614
Wilmington, DE 19801
aabga.org

Zoos and Aquariums

Zoos and aquariums provide public recreation and outdoor amusement, but more importantly, they are educational and research institutions. The educational activities of zoos and aquariums include informative exhibits for the general public, the publication of guidebooks, tours for schoolchildren, orientation programs for schoolteachers (sometimes courses are given in cooperation with local colleges so that teachers may earn credit), public lectures and films, television programs, and facilities for the use of advanced students in the study of animal behavior. The importance of these activities varies with the size and resources of the zoo or aquarium. Most are carried on at the facility, but there may be classroom follow-ups with specimens taken to schools.

The employees most often encountered by the public are the groundskeepers, zookeepers, and their assistants. Keepers engage in practical animal husbandry; recently there has been a tendency to elevate the positions professionally and to demand more training than in the past. Curators are the professional zoologists in the zoo or marine biologists at the aquarium, and positions as curators are often held by individuals who have master's or Ph.D. degrees. Curators supervise the care of the animals and make decisions on the choice of animals to display and the means used to present the displays to the public.

The zoologist or marine biologist may perform research in animal breeding, genetics, ecology, animal behavior, or other topics. He or she may need to travel to visit other facilities, to study animals in the native state, or to collect specimens. Although the most familiar animals in the zoo may be the mammals and fish at aquariums, there also must be experts on birds (ornithologists), reptiles and amphibians (herpetologists), and fish (ichthyologists). An aquarium for the study and display of fish and other aquatic creatures is often associated with a zoo, but it may be separate. Workers at zoos and aquariums find that their work never gets dull, they are relatively free from bureaucratic regulations, and their salaries are comparable with those of people of corresponding education and responsibility in local schools and colleges.

For more information, contact:

Association of Science-Technology Centers (ASTC)
1025 Vermont Avenue NW, Suite 500
Washington, D.C. 20005-3516
astc.org

Museums of Natural History

Today's natural history museums are repositories of vast databases of information about the world's existing and extinct life forms. Our interest in understanding and preserving the biodiversity of our world has resulted in the collection of information about the natural world and encouraged sharing of this information worldwide. This is why the newest members of the natural history museum staff are often bioinformatics (computer) specialists who can organize scientific information in a way that makes it easily retrievable.

Museums play an important role in transmitting scientific information to the public; hence they are of increasing significance as informal educational institutions. The most visible evidence of the museum's educational function is the exhibit. Museum exhibition as a profession has a strong appeal to certain persons, but the employment opportunities are limited. Often exhibits are prepared by staff members whose primary duties lie elsewhere, but there is an increasing tendency for museum exhibition to become a profession in its own right.

Exhibits are educational displays. Their preparation involves conception and planning, which is followed by design and execution. The exhibitor, then, is less of a specialist than are most biologists.

Not only must the person be well-grounded in general biology, he or she should especially understand systematics, ecology, and conservation. In addition, it is important to know something about the principles of three-dimensional design, color harmony, and photography. The exhibit designer will have some contact with anthropology, paleontology, geology, and geography—he or she does not need to be an expert in these fields but should have sufficient understanding of them to be able to collaborate with professionals in such disciplines.

Many museums contain classrooms, and museum personnel often collaborate with local school systems in informal instruction either in the museum or in the schools. The museum's collections are also important sources of material for instructional purposes or for scholarly research. The curator in a large natural history museum is generally a systematic biologist and has duties that are manifold. He or she occasionally makes field trips to remote areas for specimens. Once the specimen is in the museum's collection, it has to be properly identified, documented, labeled, and maintained in condition for proper use by scholars not only now but in future generations. The curator also helps in the exhibit programs, collaborates with colleagues in other institutions, gives lectures—both technical and popular—and must do scholarly research in the field and publish the results in technical journals. In many instances, the curator holds an appointment on a university faculty (some important museums are integral parts of universities) and aids in the instruction of advanced students, especially graduate students. With the increasing emphasis upon research in systematic biology, appointment or promotion to the position of curator today goes only to those who have completed the training for the Ph.D. degree.

The organization of the staff of a large museum, such as the National Museum of Natural History, a part of the Smithsonian

Institution in Washington, D.C., resembles that of a university. The areas of interest to biologists are divided into departments, such as the Department of Vertebrate Zoology, Department of Invertebrate Zoology, Department of Entomology, Department of Botany, and Department of Paleobiology. Within each department are divisions staffed by biologists of various ranks such as curators, associate curators, and assistants, reminiscent to the academic ranks of professor, associate professor, and assistant professor. Most museum directors regard their curatorial and exhibit staffs to be undermanned and seek to recruit young, trained personnel within the limits of their budgets.

Positions as assistants in natural history museums are available in limited numbers. Applicants who have bachelor's degrees with majors in biology generally fill them. Many museums have training programs for technicians, and the technical assistant may be able to obtain the formal education necessary for promotion.

The jobs available in museums do not compare in number with those in teaching, industry, or government research, but for the limited number who find employment in them, museums offer an enjoyable environment.

For more information, contact:

American Association of Museums (AAM)
1575 Eye Street NW, Suite 400
Washington, D.C. 20005
aam-us.org

Volunteer Service Organizations

You may not wish to serve in volunteer organizations as a permanent occupation, but a year or two spent in helping others may give valuable experience in addition to the satisfaction that comes from a useful job well done. There are many groups offering opportunities to be of service, and most of them do not specifically call for people with biological training. An exception is the Peace Corps, which has had many requests that can best be satisfied by individuals with biological knowledge. Peace Corps volunteers receive no salary, but transportation and health needs are cared for, and monthly allowances cover modest living costs.

Volunteers who are trained in the biosciences have served in many parts of the globe. Most of them have taught in secondary schools, in teacher training schools, or they have assisted in fieldwork. Included among the fields of biology for which there have been calls in the past are the following:

- Teachers trained in general biology, botany, and bacteriology
- Medical technologists to train hospital technicians
- Help in freshwater fisheries and fish farming
- Assistance in livestock breeding
- Entomologists to aid in pest control
- Plant pathologists for help in controlling plant diseases
- Conservation of wildlife and forests in the face of industrialization of underdeveloped countries

For more information, contact:

USA Freedom Corps
1600 Pennsylvania Avenue NW
Washington, D.C. 20500
(877) USA-CORPS

4

CAREERS IN THE BASIC BIOLOGICAL SCIENCES

GROWTH AND CHANGES in the biosciences occur at such a breathtaking pace that it is difficult to keep up with them, and some of the most promising careers are in areas that were scarcely known only a few years ago. Frederic Joliot-Curie, one of the great physicists of the early twentieth century, reportedly said that while the first half of this century belonged to the physicist, the second half would belong to the biologist. Some of the recent developments in biology, such as the human genome project, seem to bear out this prophecy. Most of these developments begin with basic research in the laboratory. While the work may seem tedious, the joy of discovery is exhilarating. Peering into microscopes and crunching data on computers, these scientists are the real explorers of what is now science fiction.

General and Systematic Biology

These are two disciplines that examine biology as whole, but in very different ways. A general biologist is someone who looks at biology in very broad terms. A professor who teaches general biology in a college or university to students who may not be science majors is fulfilling the role of general biologist, even thought he or she might have an advanced degree in a subspecialty of biology. A college graduate with a bachelor's degree in biology or even a master's degree, who has not yet chosen a special field of study, can be employed as general biologist. He or she would be expected to know how to design and perform experiments in the field or laboratory; supervise lab technicians and assistants; collect, analyze, and report data; and be very knowledgeable about all of the branches of biology without specializing in any one of them in particular.

Systematic biology—also referred to as systematics or biosystematics—is defined as the study of the classification of different kinds of organisms that exist, as well as the kinds that existed in the past and are now extinct. It includes a description and classification of organisms and of the relationship between them, as well as the changes that have occurred in them during past generations. One aspect of systematics—taxonomy—studies the appearance and structure of a plant or animal, determines how it differs from others, describes its surroundings, classifies it in its proper place in the plant or animal kingdom, and names it. The aspect of systematics concerned with how organisms change over the course of generations and what influences are at work on them is called evolution. It seeks to determine where a given species came from, what processes are acting upon it to keep it as it is or to change it into something else, and whether we can predict what forms its future may take. Systematic biologists are involved in the collection, storage, and retrieval of information on living, endangered, and extinct life forms using the latest computer technology known as bioinformatics (see Chapter 6).

Systematists are not merely concerned with appearances; they use the tools supplied by other disciplines. For example, subtle differences in the structure of DNA from one species to another may give clues of their genetic relationships. The systematist may make original observations or use data supplied by other biologists—such as physiologists—about microscopic cell structure, biochemical reactions taking place within living tissue, breeding behavior, geographical relationships, interplay between the organism and its environment, or any other information that may help to establish the position of the organism within the plant or animal kingdom.

Systematics is really a collection of many specialties, although there are a few general systematists. For example, a mycologist studies yeasts, molds, mushrooms, or other fungi. A dendrologist specializes in trees, and an algologist concentrates on the small and simple green plants known as algae. There are few jobs specifically labeled mycologist or dendrologist. Individuals with such specialized interests are biologists first of all, and they follow their specialty while teaching the usual biology courses. The American Society of Ichthyology once put it this way: "Nobody is ever hired merely to teach ichthyology . . . the young ichthyologist may . . . find that almost all of the available openings are for teachers of introductory courses like general biology." However, there are some exceptions to this. A limited number of openings for curators of ichthyology, herpetology, or other specialties do occur from time to time—mainly in such places as museums, zoos, aquariums, and fisheries laboratories.

The glamour and importance of certain fields of experimental biology, including biotechnology and some of the biomedical sciences, may have overshadowed systematic biology in the eyes of many, but it is well that we recall the enormous contributions made by systematists to the quality of life that we enjoy. There is an urgent, and indeed critical, need for a thorough understanding of biological interrelationships if our civilization is to survive. In this respect, systematics interacts with and overlaps other biological disciplines, especially ecology and genetics.

Systematists have given valuable assistance to programs designed to encourage biological control of pests and diseases. They aid in ecological studies in many ways, such as identification of organisms in water to judge the degree of water pollution. Physicians and toxicologists in hospitals and public health laboratories employ systematists as consultants to aid in the identification of such toxic plants and animals as poisonous mushrooms and snakes. They participate in the discovery of plant strains resistant to disease. They identify fossil species of plants and animals in sedimentary rocks as an essential part of oil and mineral prospecting.

Systematics involves both field and laboratory work and deals with all manner of terrestrial and aquatic habitats. Systematic biology offers opportunity to travel both in the civilized and the wild parts of the earth. Systematists also can relate their professional interests to many other technical and academic fields, including such nonscience subjects as history, logic, and classical languages.

Systematists find employment as teachers in secondary schools, colleges, universities, and agricultural colleges. Museums, botanical gardens, arboretums, zoos, aquariums, private research foundations, and various local, state, and federal agencies employ systematic biologists.

For more information, contact:

Natural Science Collections Alliance
1725 K Street NW
Washington, D.C. 20006
nscalliance.org

Microbiology

Literally speaking, the word *microbiology* means the study of the very small—that is, organisms that cannot be seen without the aid of a microscope. Microorganisms include bacteria, so bacteriology is a branch of microbiology. Many people think of bacteria as disease germs since so many infectious diseases are caused by bacteria. A closer look, however, reveals the fact that of about fifteen hundred known species of bacteria only about one hundred cause disease. Many of the other fourteen hundred are of great importance to human beings, and we could not exist without their activities.

Microorganisms, for all their tiny size and simple appearance, produce many complex substances. Some of their products are harmful, but more of them are useful substances such as vitamins and antibiotics. These include enzymes that convert complex materials into simple substances, helping in the disposal of waste and in making the materials available for reentry into the cycle of life.

Microorganisms can be studied from the point of view of taxonomy, morphology, biochemistry, physiology, ecology, genetics, or any other aspect of living things, as are higher plants and animals. Algae, fungi, yeasts, viruses, rickettsiae, and protozoa are among the kinds of organisms studied by microbiologists. Many of these appear to be simple forms of plant life, but some cannot be readily classified as either plant or animal. Protozoa, meanwhile, belong to the animal kingdom. Protozoology, a special branch of bioscience, deals with protozoa. Protozoa are important in the ecological balance: they consume bacteria, they help convert wastes into materials utilizable by higher organisms, and they are themselves consumed as an important link in the food cycle. A special group of students of protozoa are called parasitologists. A few protozoa are harmful parasites, producing such diseases as malaria, amoebic dysentery, African sleeping sickness, certain venereal diseases, and others. Not all harmful parasites are protozoa, so many parasitologists devote their attention to larger parasitic creatures, such as roundworms. Thus, a parasitologist may be partly microbiologist and partly macrobiologist.

The viruses defy simple classification as plants or animals. They are too small to be seen with an ordinary microscope or to be held back by bacteriological filters, but virologists have devised many ingenious ways of studying them. Viruses are found in the cells of bacteria, plants, and animals, and they may act as messengers, bringing in new genes. Some of the genes introduced into bacteria may alter the resistance to antibiotics. A single gene introduced into an animal cell may transform it into a cancer cell. Many plant diseases responsible for crop destruction are of viral origin. Virologists are engaged in studying all these aspects of viruses, but some are trying to turn to humans' advantage the predilection of viruses to invade animal cells and destroy them. Thus, viruses harmful to insects might replace toxic chemicals in sprays.

Microbiologists contribute a great deal to the study of genetics. Some of these studies have produced new organisms, and the United States Supreme Court has ruled that such creations are patentable. Some strains of microorganisms appear to be especially sensitive to chemical compounds capable of inducing cancer. Such compounds cause mutations in the bacteria, and this property makes it possible to detect potential carcinogens so that they can be removed from the environment.

Microbiology can boast some of the most illustrious names in the history of science and some of the greatest achievements for the benefit of human beings. Louis Pasteur, Robert Koch, Sir Alexander Fleming, and Jonas Salk are just a few of the great names that appear on the rolls of those who have contributed to microbiology. A third of all the Nobel prizes in physiology and medicine have been bestowed upon microbiologists. Microbiology has so many practical applications that some microbiologists have complained that its value as a basic science has not been properly appreciated.

Microbiologists have been responsible for the development of vaccines, antiserums, and toxoids against a wide variety of diseases in human beings and animals. These include smallpox, typhoid fever, yellow fever, whooping cough, measles, influenza, and polio. Some microbiologists hope that some day the common cold, cancer, AIDS, and others will be added to the list.

Many of our food and beverage products, including cheese, vinegar, wines and other alcoholic beverages, pickles, breads, and olive and cabbage products, to name just a few, are dependent upon microorganisms, and microbiologists have contributed to the production and improvement of all of them. Microbiologists have also developed products for the preservation of meats, vegetables, and fish, and for the tenderizing of meats. Even oil geologists use microbiological information in their prospecting.

Diseases of animals are important targets of study by microbiologists. These include both the diseases that affect the animals and those that animals can pass along to human beings. According to the World Health Organization, about 150 animal diseases are important in human medicine; such diseases, called zoonoses, include brucellosis and bovine tuberculosis, which have been conquered in most areas—but most of them remain to be controlled.

The branches of microbiology concerned with disease-producing organisms include medical microbiology and veterinary microbiology. Scientists in these areas perform research on vaccines, antiserums, and a variety of products of biological origin. A host of problems related to public health, such as the spread of infectious agents by insects, rats, or other animals; the sanitary control of water and food; and the disposal of sewage are the domain of the public health microbiologist. Agricultural microbiologists have a wide range of interests besides diseases of plants and animals, including problems such as the growth of microorganisms for use as food for human beings; yeasts and algae are among those suggested as possible future food sources.

Microbiologists teach and do research in nearly all colleges and universities and in many professional schools, including those of medicine, dentistry, public health, nursing, pharmacy, veterinary medicine, and agriculture. Private research foundations, government research laboratories and service agencies, public health facilities, hospitals, and agricultural experiment stations employ large numbers of microbiologists. Industrial microbiologists are employed by the food, chemical, and pharmaceutical industries in large numbers. These scientists are engaged in areas such as research, production, and quality control. In many instances, the large-scale production of antibiotics and other complicated molecules can be done more effectively and economically by microorganisms than by the usual methods of synthetic chemistry.

A subspecialty in the study of microbiology is mycology. A mycologist is a student of fungi. Perhaps the most familiar examples of fungi are mushrooms, but the fungi also include molds, mildews, and yeasts. Although a few fungi cause disease in human beings, the majority are of benefit. They take part in the breakdown of dead trees and other plants, helping to return the dead tissues to the soil and the air, thus completing the cycle of growth and decay. The useful products of fungal activity are many, and with genetic engineering the list is growing. Medically useful products include penicillin, streptomycin, and other antibiotics as well as steroids such as cortisone and the hormones of birth control pills. Fungi turn milk into cheese and sugar into alcohol. They are abundant in the soil, on foods, in the air, on textiles and lumber—indeed, anywhere there is organic material and moisture. They are so widespread and their metabolic products are so useful that the discovery of new fungi is an important activity of some mycologists.

Fungi and their products are being studied by many specialists in other fields, including chemists, molecular biologists, physicians, ecologists, pathologists, and engineers. Geneticists have learned much about heredity from studying the fungi, and cellular biologists and others have found much that is applicable to cancer research. In the applications of biology to forestry and agriculture, the mycologist collaborates closely with the plant pathologist, for the fungi are the chief causes of disease in higher plants.

Such professional schools as medicine, forestry, and agriculture also utilize the skills of mycologists. Medical research laboratories, whether in private research institutes, in the pharmaceutical industry, or in installations of the public health service, employ mycologists. In such institutions, fungi are studied for their value in producing antibiotics and other medically useful products in ways that chemists cannot economically duplicate in the test tube. Industries and laboratories interested in food production, leather, textiles, and forestry products also have need of mycologists. Chemical manufacturers seek to discover means of preventing spoilage of manufactured goods by devising and testing chemical substances that will control or kill fungal growth; mycologists are employed for testing such substances.

Thus, the man or woman trained in microbiology can have his or her choice of many careers. That training will involve basic courses in biology, chemistry, mathematics, and physics. Some colleges permit a major in microbiology; elective courses in microbiology and related subjects may vary depending upon the student's specific interest. If it is agricultural microbiology, the student will need botany and plant pathology, for example. If he or she is headed toward the chemical industries, a course in chemical engineering might be appropriate.

The top jobs in research and in university teaching will be held by those possessing doctoral degrees, as in most of the biosciences; but the variety of jobs available for microbiologists opens up many opportunities for those with baccalaureate degrees as well.

For more information, contact:

American Society for Microbiology (ASM)
1752 N Street NW
Washington, D.C. 20036
asm.org

Mycological Society of America (MSA)
(no headquarters office)
msafungi.org

Botany and Plant Science Specialties

There are many varieties of botanists, the portion of biologists who are especially interested in plants. Plant systematists or taxonomists describe, classify, and study the evolutionary interrelationships of the nearly endless variety of members of the plant kingdom. Plant morphologists are fascinated by the form and structure of plants; plant ecologists with their environmental relationships. There are no hard and fast lines between these various specialties. It is clear that the systematist must have an understanding of morphology and ecology. Plant physiologists are primarily concerned with the normal functioning and behavior of plants, how the plant absorbs energy and what it does with it, for example. The highly important problems of plant disease engage the attention of the phytopathologist (or plant pathologist). Some botanists specialize in certain groups of plants; for example, the bryologist studies mosses and liverworts, and the dendrologist concentrates on trees. Other plant scientists use their training in practical applications of their skills; they may become foresters, horticulturists, or agricultural scientists. Careers in botany, then, may be quite varied.

Plant Physiology

The increasing population of the earth will make continually greater demands upon our ability to control the growth and development of plants for improved food production; the plant physiologist is one of the key persons in this struggle. A large percentage of the efforts of plant physiologists is devoted to the study of plant metabolism, including photosynthesis, as well as the mechanisms by which the plant absorbs and transports water and minerals. Knowledge of the utilization of water by plants would be valuable in those parts of the world where water is a precious commodity in short supply. The increasing uses of water for industry in our own country and the resulting effects upon the reservoir of underground water stresses the importance of learning the role of plants in the overall cycle of water. More thorough knowledge of mineral metabolism in plants could help in learning how various plants adapt to soil of differing mineral content. Of course, a better understanding of photosynthesis might help immeasurably in increasing the manufacture of basic food substances; at the present time, only plants are able to make them.

One expanding facet of plant physiology is that of environmental physiology. The increased air pollution of recent years has exposed plants to gases and particulate matters for which they were not adapted, and there have been many instances of injuries to plants from these sources, both economic and aesthetic. The sources include the burning of fossil fuels, incomplete combustion of coal or wood, and a great variety of industrial emissions. Injuries appear whenever a certain concentration is exceeded; different species of plants respond to different concentrations and exhibit different signs and symptoms. The identification of the trouble is a highly specialized field. In these studies, the plant physiologist, the ecologist, and the meteorologist cooperate with one another.

The solution to these unsolved problems relating to plant physiology will be sought by those plant physiologists who are engaged in basic research, but there are also many involved in applying basic concepts to practical applications. About two-thirds of all plant physiologists work in universities, most dividing their time between teaching and research. The remainder is employed in government laboratories, in industry, or by private research foundations. The American Society of Plant Physiologists has estimated that research in plant physiology is about equally divided between basic and applied. Plant physiologists interested in applied research find many ways in which their chosen science is of practical benefit. If they are in industry, for example, they may help to develop new chemicals or new ways of using chemicals for such things as controlling plant growth, increasing plant production, or destroying weeds.

The plant physiologist may deal with organic chemistry, physics, genetics, plant pathology, molecular biology, and other disciplines, but the job is to analyze and coordinate this knowledge. The plant physiologist may deal with a small part of the plant, but the ultimate goal is the understanding of the entire organism. It is no wonder that plant physiologists are found in all sections of the country, in every major university, and in all the agricultural research centers.

The education and training of plant physiologists do not differ markedly from those of other biologists during the undergraduate years. Although a basic understanding of biology is necessary, some plant physiologists have expressed the view that the physical sciences—mathematics, chemistry, and physics—are so important that physical science majors make good candidates for concentration on biological studies in graduate school leading to an advanced degree in plant physiology. There are, of course, many jobs in places such as plants' physiology laboratories and greenhouses that do not require advanced degrees, but those with doctorates usually hold the top jobs.

It may be seen that plant physiology forms a connecting link between basic biological research on the one hand and agriculture, forestry, and similar applied disciplines on the other. Biologists trained in this field will find a variety of outlets for their talents.

Plant Pathology

While the plant physiologist contributes discoveries that enable us to understand plant growth, development, and behavior with corresponding improvements in food production, the plant pathologist provides knowledge that enables us to control the plant diseases that continually threaten to wipe out all the gains made by agriculture, horticulture, forestry, and similar disciplines. The success or failure of the plant pathologist determines not only how well we eat, but whether we can survive.

Plant diseases cause billions of dollars in losses every year—bacteria, fungi, viruses, and other pathogens attack fruits, grains, vegetables, flowers, and animals. The tools that will be employed to meet these challenges will include the breeding of plants resistant to disease and the use of chemicals, including antibiotics and plant hormones, for combating disease. The plant pathologist thus cooperates with the plant physiologist, the biochemist, and others.

The American Phytopathological Society has estimated that there are more than fifty thousand destructive plant diseases. This science is growing in importance and plant pathologists find employment in many diverse areas. Courses in plant pathology are offered in universities in every state and in Puerto Rico. Teachers trained in plant pathology are employed in teaching such courses not only in departments of plant pathology but also in other biology departments, as well as in agricultural schools, in extension courses, and sometimes in secondary schools.

Research positions are available in state agricultural experiment stations as well as in the U.S. Department of Agriculture and in some other government departments, including the Foreign Service.

All major industrial firms engaged in the production of agricultural chemicals employ plant pathologists, and the federal government's program of technical aid to foreign nations engages many plant pathologists. Other phytopathologists work in conservation projects. These may be in wide-open spaces, ranges, national parks, and forests, or in cities working with grasses, trees, flowers, and ornamental plants. Some are becoming freelancers; that is, they go into private practice as consultants on plant disease or start up their own services for testing or disease control. They are doctors of plant disease, just as veterinarians are doctors of animal disease, or physicians are doctors of human disease. Their numbers are small, but growing.

There are positions in plant pathology for those with diverse levels of education. A baccalaureate degree in plant pathology is offered by some schools whose graduates find jobs with food processors, manufacturers of agricultural chemicals, and similar employers. They also may become federal or state plant inspectors, or they may teach in secondary schools or in two-year colleges. Those who continue their education through the doctorate will be equipped to handle the most challenging problems in the field and to qualify for the highest positions. The person who chooses plant pathology will be in a position to help humanity and all the animal kingdom in the process of helping the members of the plant kingdom.

For more information, contact:

Botanical Society of America
P.O. Box 299
St. Louis, MO 63166-0299
botany.org

Zoology

Zoology is the study of animals, including protozoa, jellyfish, worms, snails, insects, fishes, amphibians, reptiles, birds, and mammals. Historically, it has been one of the most popular branches of biology. Zoologists work in the field and in the laboratory with all sorts of high technology, including DNA identification, and they develop databanks of information that capture data on some animals that are now extinct. They study not only animals, but also their habitats and threats to their survival such as acid rain, deforestation, and global warming. Some zoologists choose to specialize in agriculture or food science. Zoologists often go on to pursue subspecialty research that focuses on one aspect of zoology, such as marine biology or entomology.

When you first saw the heading for this section, you probably thought that it would be about people who work in zoos. And they do! But pharmaceutical companies, the food industry, breweries, biotechnology companies, and utilities, petroleum, and forest industries also employ zoologists. Their duties often include advising their employers or clients on the humane treatment of laboratory animals and the selection of species that are appropriate for the laboratory. The environmental impact of an industry such as lumbering or energy production from a nuclear power plant can also be determined by an expert in zoology.

If you are talented in the communication arts or enjoy acting, there are many opportunities for writing about animal life, and media productions about the natural sciences are among the most popular on television.

For more information, contact:

Canadian Society of Zoologists
www3.uqar.uquebec.ca/jpellerin/csz/cszanglais/index.htm

Entomology

More than three-fourths of all the species of animals in the world today are insects or their close relatives. From the point of view of human beings, many pests spread disease, compete for food, or destroy desirable plants. Others, however, are useful in that they pollinate trees, crops, and other plants; provide food for us; or help to destroy pest species. Whichever they do, insects affect the lives of every person. Entomologists are the biologists who study them.

Entomology overlaps with many other biological disciplines. Although the description and classification of insect forms have been going on for more than a century and hundreds of thousands of insects have been described and named, scientists estimate that there may be as many as ten million types of insects that have not yet been discovered. The identification and classification of insects are fundamental to all other research in entomology.

The insect physiologist makes discoveries that are useful in many areas—sometimes even in human medicine. An important part of research in entomology is the study of insect control; that is, research aimed at reducing or eliminating the harm done by insect pests. The economic entomologist is especially concerned with reducing the damage done by insects to crops, forests, food in storage, and other interests of people.

In the past, most attention has been paid to insect control by means of poisonous chemicals, so the work of the entomologist has overlapped with that of the toxicologist. Now many are interested in the use of chemical substances that are not systemic poisons: they might produce abnormal growth or behavior of the insects, they might attract insects to traps, or they might render insects sterile so they cannot reproduce. These goals are helped by research on the physiology, reproduction, and behavior of insects, and the knowledge gained in this research is often of interest in other fields of animal and human biology.

Another avenue of approach to insect control is known as biological control. This involves the study of other insects or other forms of life that prey upon or destroy the insects we regard as pests, as well as the study of insect diseases—bacteria, viruses, or fungi that attract insects. The work of the entomologist thus may be closely linked with that of the microbiologist, the virologist, or the mycologist. No form of life can be destroyed without affecting the balance of nature. Hence the entomologist engaged in insect control will have occasion to collaborate with the ecologist and the wildlife biologist.

It would be difficult to mention a field of biology offering a greater variety of employment opportunities than entomology. Most teachers of entomology are hired by colleges and universities—especially colleges of agriculture and veterinary medicine. Industries that employ entomologists include producers and processors of food, the chemical industry interested in chemicals for insect control, and the lumber and pulp industries, which utilize the skills of forest entomologists. We see constant reminders to help prevent forest fires, but few realize that insects destroy more timber each year than do forest fires.

The production and storage of food and fiber is of the utmost urgency for the expanding world population—now increasing by about 1.6 percent annually, which would mean that the world population will double by the year 2028. Meeting this challenge would be greatly simplified if insect damage were eradicated, for it has been estimated that insects destroy fully one-third of all production. Success or failure in controlling insects could well make the difference between starvation and survival in much of the world, especially in developing countries. Along with this, insect-borne diseases make life miserable for millions, and indeed the areas at present that are uninhabitable or nearly so would be accessible if the insects could be controlled.

There are tremendous challenges in entomological research, but the application of research findings also offers many employment opportunities and is of immense importance. For example, in agriculture, knowledge gained by the research scientist is transmitted by extension workers to farmers. The research findings are also passed on to the next generation by teachers. The private sector employs many people with skills in entomology. Major chemical companies employ entomologists skilled in toxicology and insect control. Although in the past mistakes have been made in the application of pesticides, there is growing realization that skilled personnel are greatly needed in devising and applying a balanced system of pest management. In addition to agricultural pests, there is a large industry in the United States engaged in control of termites and other pests that attack dwellings and other structures.

The demand for skills in the control of pests is great. Employment as a technician in pest control does not require a college degree, but some specialized education is needed for advancement, and both two-year associate degrees and four-year baccalaureate degrees in pest control may be obtained. Some of this training is available by correspondence.

Many entomologists are employed by state and federal governments in research laboratories and in biological survey work. Others are extension entomologists, helping farmers, growers, nursery workers, and home owners wherever insects present problems in everyday living and commerce. Health agencies employ medical entomologists—that is, those specializing in insects responsible for the spread of disease. Agriculture experiment stations, plant inspection agencies, mosquito control boards, conservation agencies, and museums are a few of the other sources of employment opportunities. Several hundred inspectors are employed by the Animal and Plant Health Inspection Service of the U.S. Department of Agriculture to identify pests that hitchhike to the United States on imported animals and in tourists' pockets. These entomological inspectors perform an important and useful service. For example, inspectors have intercepted bark beetles that help spread Dutch elm disease and wood-borers in crating and packing material, as well as fruit hidden in flight luggage containing larvae of fruit flies capable of threatening an entire industry such as citrus growing.

The largest organization of professional entomologists is the Entomological Society of America, with about ninety-two hundred members. The society encourages the highest standards among its members, promotes communication of information, and maintains a permanent office that answers inquiries about educational requirements and job opportunities.

For more information, contact:

Entomological Society of America
9301 Annapolis Road, Suite 300
Lanham, MD 20706-3115
entsoc.org

Marine (Oceanography) and Aquatic Biology

Some biologists find fascination in a study of the classification, mode of life, functions, or adaptations of organisms inhabiting the sea—marine biology—or freshwater—aquatic biology. Few biologists will have interests broad enough to cover all these aspects thoroughly. One may be especially interested in the physiology of fish, another in the systematics of marine algae, yet another in the structure or embryology of a particular group, for example, the minute invertebrate animals that form a part of the plankton (the small floating or swimming forms that are the basis of the food chain for all the larger creatures).

For many years, numerous observers have foreseen serious food shortages in widespread areas of the earth, and some have forecast worldwide famine. There is no question that the population is increasing faster than agricultural production in the world as a whole. Marine biology may offer one bright spot in this gloomy picture. Food from aquatic and marine organisms contributes protein, vitamins, and minerals to human nutrition—the very essentials that people in developing countries need the most. This need can be satisfied only by the results of continuing research efforts by marine and aquatic biologists.

Relying upon fishing to produce needed food is equivalent to the method of prehistoric people. The aquatic equivalent to agriculture is aquaculture, and only through this procedure can we realize the full potential of aquatic organisms. Aquaculture has begun to assume an important role in the United States as many large firms have entered the field. However, the fledgling industry still produces only about three hundred million pounds of food annually, which accounts for about 8 percent of America's seafood consumption.

Energy conversion by water-dwelling animals is far more efficient than by land animals; that is, for each pound of food energy they consume, a greater portion of it is converted to meat suitable for human food. The explanation for this remarkable circumstance is twofold: temperatures in the water environment do not fluctuate wildly as they do in the air; hence aquatic organisms do not have to waste much energy in combating cold or in cooling their bodies during hot spells. In addition, the water they live in weighs nearly the same as does an equal volume of their own bodies; therefore they do not need to spend large amounts of energy for antigravity purposes.

For these reasons, the yields achieved in water far outstrip those on land. Fertilized catfish ponds in the southern part of our country may yield as many as 4,500 pounds of fish per acre per year. This figure is dwarfed by the crops harvested from salt water. Some figures quoted by workers in ocean research laboratories range from 51,000 pounds of meat per acre annually in Japanese oyster beds to the fantastic figure of 268,000 pounds per acre per year in Spanish mussel colonies. To give some idea to the meaning of these figures, consider that a good yield of small grain on a farm may be on the order of 100 bushels per acre. At 60 pounds per bushel, this would be about 6,000 pounds of grain per acre. When this is fed to animals for producing meat, it will yield about 600 pounds of unprocessed meat.

The full potential of aquaculture cannot be realized without the contributions to knowledge that only the biologist can supply. For example, the biosystematist could study the relationships of the species concerned and perhaps find useful species that are not yet used for food. The systematist also would be in a position to study the many lowly members of the food chain in order to provide most effectively the food for the species being cultivated. The systematist also could supply information to aid the geneticist in selecting species for hybridization, and the geneticist would supervise selective breeding and hybridization. A program at the University of Washington in Seattle using rainbow trout as a subject produced a breed that grows to a weight of six to seven pounds in the time it takes an ordinary trout to grow to six or seven ounces. This new breed also tolerates water temperatures that the wild trout cannot endure.

There are many unsolved problems in aquaculture. For example, although oysters and shrimp are widely cultivated, experiments are needed on the genetics of these creatures. Techniques for growing lobster and abalone have recently been developed, but some companies have found attempts at cultivation of several species of seafood animals to be unprofitable, and some have given up attempts. Others, however, are very successful. Thus the need for additional research is apparent. Studies of the physiology of marine invertebrates need to be done. Such studies would include nutrition and food supply for the animals under study, reproductive and endocrine physiology, the diseases that might threaten the venture, and all other aspects of their lives.

From this discussion, it is clear that there is plenty of work to be done by anybody choosing marine or aquatic biology for a career, and the potential for aid to humanity is great. Aquaculture, however, is only a special application of marine biology and is by no means the only source of career opportunities in these fields. Departments of oceanography in universities conduct studies in marine biology as well as in the chemistry, physics, and geology of the marine environment. The biologists in such departments are concerned with all aspects of the systematics, biochemistry, and physiology of plants and animals in water. Many departments of botany and zoology also employ biologists interested in aquatic and marine organisms. Institutions and agencies interested in the impact of society's pollution tendencies upon watery habitats also offer employment opportunities. These effects are often difficult to study because of the exceedingly complex effects of currents in bays, fjords, estuaries, and in the open sea and streams. The biologist with a good foundation in mathematics and in computer technology is in a particularly good position to tackle these difficult problems.

Marine and aquatic biology offers a seemingly unending variety of occupations, and with advances in technology the list of possible careers expands. There are opportunities for outdoor occupations and a wide variety of indoor employment, or a mix of the two. A sample of the openings that have been filled within recent years include:

- Monitoring salmon migration for a state agency
- Inspecting fish handling aboard a processing vessel
- Serving as agent for the marine advisory service of NOAA (National Oceanic and Atmospheric Administration)
- Analyzing water samples for culture of shellfish
- Managing fish hatcheries
- Surveying fish population
- Supervising a fish farm
- Investigating effects of volcanic eruptions on lakes and rivers
- Preparing environmental impact statements
- Managing a stream for a private club

An especially active field with many job openings deals with the handling and processing of fish and shellfish for human consumption. These openings require knowledge of food science as well as marine biology. Food technologists in this field may be involved not only with the familiar food fish such as salmon and cod, but also with species available for food but not much utilized—such as shark, squid, alewives, and eels.

Agencies of the U.S. government that employ those trained in fisheries science include:

Department of the Interior
    U.S. Fish and Wildlife Service
    National Park Service
    Bureau of Reclamation

Department of Commerce
  National Oceanic and Atmospheric Administration
Department of Agriculture
  Farmers Home Administration
  Forest Service
  Soil Conservation Service
State Department
  Bureau of Oceans and International Environmental and
    Scientific Affairs

Some international agencies, such as the Food and Agriculture Organization of the United Nations, also employ marine biologists. Special laboratories devoted to research in marine and aquatic biology are located on the Atlantic, Pacific, and Gulf Coasts, and some are inland. A few are independent, such as the well-known Marine Biological Laboratory at Woods Hole, Massachusetts. Others are connected with universities, such as the Rosenstiel School of Marine and Atmospheric Sciences at the University of Miami and the Scripps Institute of Oceanography of the University of California at San Diego. Some university laboratories are located in close proximity with other agencies; for example, the College of Ocean and Fishery Sciences of the University of Washington in Seattle includes a School of Fisheries that offers undergraduate degrees in fisheries science or in food science. Nearby is a laboratory operated by the State Fisheries Department as well as the Northwest and Alaska Fisheries Center of the National Oceanic and Atmospheric Administration of the U.S. Department of Commerce.

These institutions and others like them offer careers to biologists primarily interested in research. In those supported by universities there are ample opportunities for teaching as well as for those who enjoy routine technical work, such as chemical analysis or plankton sampling. Some of these institutions support oceangoing research vessels—floating laboratories that range all over the world and offer especially interesting opportunities for a limited number of biologists. Areas of research in marine biology make a long list; they may embrace ecology, water quality studies, culture of organisms for food for fishes as well as culture of fish, physiology, pathology, limnology, computer modeling, and many other specialties.

The person considering marine or aquatic biology has a wide choice of colleges and universities where education and training can be obtained. Some schools offer undergraduate programs in fisheries science, but the American Fisheries Society emphasizes that before specializing, students should first obtain a thorough background in biology, including anatomy, microbiology, genetics, and biochemistry. Mathematics, computer science, and statistics also should be included, and one must not forget communication skills, English, and the humanities. Sometimes there are opportunities for summer jobs, which not only provide valuable educational experience, but also will help the student decide whether this is a career he or she wishes to pursue. There are more than a hundred colleges and universities offering courses related to fisheries sciences at the undergraduate level. They include subjects such as fisheries biology, fisheries management, freshwater biology, fish physiology, fish genetics, fish behavior, fish diseases, water quality management, and many others. The American Fisheries Society maintains a list of educational institutions offering such courses.

Although the most challenging career opportunities in marine biology research are available primarily to those with advanced degrees, there are large numbers of positions open for those interested in practical applications. Several commentators have urged that the exploration of the inner space of the earth's oceans be given a priority at least as great as the glamorous exploration of outer space. As the importance of knowledge of the seas becomes more widely recognized, career opportunities in marine science, both biological and physical, will continue to increase.

For more information, contact:

American Society of Limnology and Oceanography
ASLO Business Office
5400 Bosque Boulevard, Suite 680
Waco, TX 76710-4496
aslo.org

Ecology and Wildlife Biology

Ecology, the study of the interaction between living things and their environment, is not new but has recently assumed an importance in the popular mind not previously accorded to it. With the vastly increasing impact that people have had on the environment, it is important for our survival that we understand what we are doing to the world in which we live. The future of our species depends upon maintaining a balanced harmony with nature.

The extinction of the dinosaurs was a very impressive event in geological history, but if we reflect that a thousand species of dinosaurs became extinct over a period of a million years, we can see that on the average only one form disappeared in each one thousand years. By contrast, activities by human beings have destroyed more than two hundred species of birds and mammals within the past two or three centuries. Many others have been so drastically reduced in numbers that they may be doomed in spite of efforts to save them. It is not necessary to destroy the last member of a species to eliminate it, for there is a certain critical level below which a species fails to reproduce.

History is replete with examples, both ancient and modern, of adverse effects upon human culture when the principles of ecology are flaunted. The environment was able to absorb everything that we could do to it so long as technology was in a relatively primitive state and our numbers were not too great. But now it is threatened with a technology that even includes the potential of destroying all life. Moreover, if the increase in the rate of population growth is not curbed, it will render ineffective all other efforts at preservation of an environment in which most of us would like to live.

Some of the problems addressed by the ecologist, then, are of basic importance, and many international programs are heavily oriented toward ecological problems. Ecologists often need to know some fields other than their specialty; for example, to understand the concentrations of chemicals in rivers or lakes and their effects upon a community, ecologists may need to have general and special knowledge of some aspects of chemistry and of social sciences. If called upon to prepare environmental impact statements, ecologists will need all of these plus communication skills. The Ecological Society of America has stated that the demand for ecologists will continue as long as environmental problems and issues persist.

Although some ecologists are engaged in research, for many teaching is a basic function. Private industry and government use many ecologists as consultants. Consulting may utilize practical application of the ecologist's special skills, involving interactions with people of many professions, including economists, lawyers, planning personnel, as well as other scientists. In addition to the usual courses in chemistry, physics, and mathematics that all biology majors should have, a study of soil science, climatology, basic statistics, computer science, and geology is recommended.

Teachers who are oriented toward ecology may find employment in secondary schools as well as collegiate institutions. University departments that hire ecologists include the usual bioscience departments—biology, botany, zoology, and microbiology—and also specialized departments, such as forestry, fisheries, biology, horticulture, agronomy, entomology, oceanography, and wildlife management; there are also interdisciplinary programs. In the federal government, the Forest Service, Soil Conservation Service, National Park Service, Fish and Wildlife Service, and U.S. Public Health Service are examples of agencies that utilize the skills of ecologists. Environmental organizations such as The Sierra Club, National Audubon Society, and Greenpeace rely on the expertise and activism of ecologists. The manufacturers of agricultural products, especially fertilizers and insecticides, hire ecologically oriented personnel, as do the members of the paper and oil industries where pollution is a problem. Several agencies of the United Nations have employed ecologists to gather data relating to the human environment in many parts of the world. Other ecologists have served as advisers.

From this discussion, it should be clear that ecologists are vitally interested in conservation. Special careers in wildlife conservation are available. The wildlife biologist aids in the management of game, fish, fowl, fur-bearing animals, or any type of wildlife. The biologist is interested in the habitats of all these animals and may help in the preservation or restoration of streams, lakes, or marshes. Sometimes the work takes the wildlife biologist into remote areas, often under rugged and difficult field conditions. Other wildlife biologists may work in laboratories, concentrate on teaching, take part in extension work, or write or give lectures in their specialty. The research that wildlife biologists do may be related to taxonomy, physiology, genetics, and many other fields as applied to wild animals, fish, or birds. The research may be of a basic scientific nature or have practical applications.

Most of the work of the wildlife biologist will be directed toward learning as much as possible about wild animals so as to preserve their existence and to lessen the impact of our civilization upon them. The biologist who chooses to devote his or her time and talents to ecology, conservation, and wildlife biology will be rewarded not only by a fascinating study, but by the knowledge that his or her future and that of humankind are intimately bound. Ecologists and wildlife biologists are prominently involved in studies on the environmental aspects of the search for new sources of energy. Among their concerns are aid in the proper design, location, and operating methods of power plants; the effects of high voltage on wildlife; and the development of old mining land into a suitable habitat for wildlife. Whether you are of an idealistic or a practical nature, you may find these challenges to be rewarding.

For more information, contact:

Ecological Society of America
1707 H Street NW, Suite 400
Washington, D.C. 20006-3915
esa.org

Genetics

The study of genetics pervades almost every field of biology today. Simply defined, genetics is the science of heredity. Its pursuit involves observation of the superficial appearance of an animal or plant as related to its parents or its offspring, the inheritance of biochemical characteristics, the intimate nature of the structures in cells—especially the sex cells—that transmit heritable traits, and all other aspects of the complex mechanisms involved in heredity.

The work that individual geneticists do varies from the solution of highly abstract and theoretical problems to the application of genetic principles to practical and economically important subjects. Any species of plant, animal, or microorganism may serve as the object for the geneticist's scrutiny. Much of what is known about cellular mechanisms involved in the transmission of traits from one generation to another has been gathered from the study of relatively simple forms of life, such as bacteria and yeasts. The lowly fruit fly, *Drosophila*, has probably contributed more than any other animal to knowledge of the cellular structures known as chromosomes and genes, which are involved in heredity. Among higher plants, probably more is known about the genetics of corn than of any other plant.

Human genetics has been widely studied, too, including hereditary traits, hereditary diseases, and the interrelationship between inherited characteristics and their modification by the environment. There are, however, many gaps in our knowledge.

Genetics has conferred many varied practical benefits upon humankind. The great hybrid corn industry, which has added millions of bushels to the annual crop of that important food, owes its existence to the study of the genetics of the corn plant. Developments in the genetics of crops, especially rice, have contributed greatly to the widely heralded green revolution that has increased the production of the staple food so important to the millions of people in Southeast Asia. Perhaps further advances will lessen the dependence of these new varieties on the use of massive amounts of fertilizer and pesticides.

The selective breeding that has produced superior strains of livestock is a practical application of genetics. Several years ago a parasitic fly, the screw-worm fly, threatened to wipe out the cattle industry in Florida; the larva of this fly feeds upon the living tissues of cattle. Geneticists (and other biologists) virtually eliminated the fly from the entire cattle growing area by the simple expedient of releasing large numbers of male screw-worm flies that had been rendered sterile by radiation. Since the female screw-worm fly mates but once, a mating with a sterile male prevents the laying of fertile eggs. It does not necessarily follow that a similar treatment would eliminate all pests, but a study of the biology, including the mechanisms of heredity, of all species would contribute greatly to the solution of the problems that they present.

Opportunities for additional contributions of genetics are abundant. Further improvements in food crops and in breeds of domestic animals will help solve food problems. Better knowledge of hereditary diseases also is needed. Genetic studies of endless variety are in progress.

Although many advances in genetics have been possible by experiments in the crossbreeding of plants and animals, many opportunities are opening up in areas that owe their existence to the startling advances made by molecular biology. Information has accumulated in such volume and at such a rate that new agencies are being formed for the storage and subsequent retrieval of data in gene banks. The units of heredity, the genes, are made up of only four units or molecules—adenine, cytosine, guanine, and thymine, abbreviated as A, C, G, T—repeated over and over hundreds or thousands of times in varying sequence such as ACGTAGT-CATGC . . . The human genome, or the sum of all the genes in a single set of human chromosomes, is said to contain about three and a half billion such units. As the sequence of each new gene is determined, it can be compared with information already in the data bank.

Some of the applications of genetics have aroused misgivings. For example, some people have expressed the fear that geneticists might inadvertently create new species of dangerous organisms.

This problem has been discussed in conferences held by the scientists involved in such research, and they have agreed that they must act responsibly. In fact, there seems to be no indication that the worst fears expressed at the beginning of this research will be realized. Another source of unease is genetic testing of employees by employers. Some genetic traits might make certain employees predisposed to illness when they are exposed to certain chemicals, for example. Others might suffer genetic damage from exposure, which could be detected by monitoring, so genetic testing could possibly be used not only to screen prospective workers, but to detect any genetic changes after employment. Some have regarded this as an invasion of privacy or as a possible means of discrimination if the practice is misused. However, the use of genetic testing is a growing practice, so employment opportunities for geneticists skilled in this area are increasing.

Industrial concerns employing geneticists also include pharmaceutical manufacturers; large producers of seed, especially hybrid seed corn; large producers of livestock and poultry; and large fur-breeding farms. Government laboratories that traditionally employ geneticists include the Department of Agriculture, the Fish and Wildlife Service, the National Institutes of Health, and many others. Agricultural colleges employ not only theoretical geneticists but also those concerned with practical applications in the management of livestock, poultry, or crops. They usually spend part of their time teaching and part carrying out research programs. Some universities have separate departments of genetics, but most of the employment opportunities in colleges and universities are in departments such as biology, botany, zoology, or microbiology.

From this discussion, it is clear that genetics offers a variety of careers for those prepared to take advantage of the opportunities. A background in biology, chemistry, physics, mathematics, and computer technology would be helpful in giving the individual the widest choices.

For more information, contact:

American Society for Human Genetics (ASHG)
9650 Rockville Pike
Bethesda, MD 20814
faseb.org/genetics/ashg

Exobiology

Exobiology is the study of life outside of the planet Earth, or extra-terrestrial life. Since we are not sure that there is life as we know it on other planets, exobiologists develop ways to search for it. When an astronaut performs a scientific experiment during a mission, he or she is often testing for life signs and in that role acts as an exobiologist.

Also known as "astrobiology," this is one of the smallest branches of biology. Most of the scientists who are very active in this field of research work for the National Aeronautic and Space Administration (NASA). There are about fifty staff members on NASA's exobiology team. About three hundred scientists from all over the globe share their findings about life outside our world by interacting at the International Society for the Study of the Origin of Life. Since little is known about life in outer space, these scientists study the conditions that caused life to form on Earth, otherwise known as evolution. These conditions were replicated in 1953, in an experiment conducted by two scientists named Miller and Urey in a laboratory at the University of Chicago. Several gases that could have been the prehistoric building blocks of life were added to a glass chamber that was then exposed to an electrical current that simulated lightning strikes. The result was amino acids that are the basic components of cells. Since then, the experiments have gotten more sophisticated, but these building blocks of life are what astrobiologists look for when investigating new worlds for possible life. Their investigations also focus on the future of life on earth and in the universe. This is a very multidisciplinary field of study that involves more than experts in biology. NASA's lead teams are groups of scientists who are working on understanding life in the universe. There are also international partners who share information with NASA to enhance its exobiology research efforts. If you have an interest in extraterrestrial life and are a team player, this might be the niche for you.

For more information, contact:

Exobiology Branch, Code SSX
Mail Stop 239-4
Moffett Field, CA 94035
exobiology.arc.nasa.gov

5

CAREERS IN THE BIOMEDICAL SCIENCES

BIOLOGISTS WHO CHOOSE to work in one of the biomedical sciences find themselves at the very forefront of advances in knowledge of health and disease, in factors governing aging, and in improvements in the physical and mental well-being of humanity. Nearly all medical advances have been based upon observations previously made in the laboratory of the bioscientist. The discoveries made in these laboratories have applications not only in medicine, but also in many other fields of benefit to society.

As we have seen in the other biological sciences, the impact of bioinformatics and genomics has revolutionized research and practice. In the biomedical sciences, this may someday translate into a computerized remedy for cancer or for other deadly diseases as our family physicians match our genetic codes with that of cures.

Physiology

The interests of physiologists are so varied that it is difficult to define physiology. It is usual to consider physiology as being the science concerned with the functions and operations of a living being or any of its parts, and of the interrelationship between one living part and another. In a sense, all the biomedical sciences to be discussed in this chapter may be considered as branches of physiology, or they developed into independent disciplines from physiological origins but can still be considered to be part of the general category of physiological sciences.

Physiologists study living creatures, including people themselves. The results of such inquiries form the very basic structure of medicine, whether human or veterinary. Scientists in related disciplines—such as biochemistry, pharmacology, biophysics, and psychology—must have a background in physiology. Although the information gained by the study of animals most closely resembling human beings—that is, mammals—has the most obvious application to human physiology, much has been learned from observations of creatures far removed from the human on the evolutionary scale.

One particularly interesting example of a physiological study concerns a physiologist who studied for many years the water balance in frogs; that is, the intake and output of water by the body of the animal. One might inquire what the practical use of such an activity could be. To the scientist, such a question may seem irrelevant, and the experiments may have been done simply as a response to the need of the human mind to know. But in this instance, the simple experiments in the frogs were destined to lead in many directions. Other physiologists took up the study and discovered that the electrical and chemical forces involved in transporting water and salt through frog skin could also be involved in the functioning of nerve cells and the kidneys in human beings. After many further steps, these investigations, in turn, were eventually put to practical use by physicians wishing to regulate kidney output in patients who had certain kinds of heart disease. But that is not all. The knowledge gained in these studies has also proved to be invaluable in aiding people to cope with desert conditions; much use was made of it in the desert campaigns in North Africa during World War II.

Although there are some general physiologists, most physiologists specialize, and the list of specialties is a long one. The cellular physiologist studies processes that go on within the microscopic world of individual cells. The cells may range from bacterial cells to those derived from human tissues, and information learned from one form often (though not always) applies to many others. In this way, laws that govern vital processes are discovered.

Other physiologists may become engrossed in the functioning of some particular organ of the body or a system of organs. For example, a physiologist who studies the endocrine system is an endocrinologist; her or his specialty is the system of glands that release secretions into the bloodstream to be carried to other organs and assist in the regulation of growth, metabolism, reproduction, and many other processes. Even an endocrinologist may specialize and may concentrate on, for example, the reproductive system. Some physiologists study particular groups of animals such as insects, fishes, or even protozoa. The comparative physiologist is interested in those aspects in which one form differs from another; these findings are especially valuable to the veterinary physician as well as to the stockbreeder or the pet fancier. You might find an exciting challenge as an environmental physiologist who can make direct and immediate contributions to our knowledge and awareness of the effect of society's changes in the environment, as well as of exposure to unusual stresses, such as certain tropical regions, the arctic, high altitudes, or space. It is not our intention to list all the kinds of physiologists there are, but merely to indicate by a few examples the surprising diversity available to you if you are considering physiological science.

The level of education you need as a physiologist depends largely upon what position in the physiological team you want to assume. There are many openings for laboratory assistants and technicians. Such positions may sometimes be entered directly from high school or perhaps with an associate in arts degree from a two-year college. However, for a more advanced position in physiology, a more prolonged education is necessary, and those with Ph.D. or M.D. degrees hold the top-notch jobs in physiology.

Colleges and universities employ about two-thirds of all physiologists. They are engaged in teaching, research, or both. Not all colleges have departments of physiology; at the undergraduate level of teaching, most physiologists have appointments in departments such as biology, zoology, and entomology. Agricultural, dental, and veterinary schools also employ physiologists. Medical schools are especially important, for physiology is the very foundation of medicine, and physiologists are employed not only in departments of physiology and other basic sciences, but often in clinical departments—medicine, surgery—as well. Clinics, hospitals, private research foundations, drug companies, U.S. government laboratories and regulatory agencies—these and many others employ physiologists.

From time to time, the American Physiological Society surveys the educational institutions of the United States, Canada, and Mexico and lists all those offering degrees in physiology. It should be emphasized, however, that the future physiologist's choice of a college is by no means limited to one that offers an undergraduate major in physiology. Indeed, the majority of physiologists now at the height of their careers specialized in physiology only in graduate school. A good background in biological science, however, is essential. This will include both general and advanced biology, physics, and general, organic, analytical, and physical chemistry. In recent years, the importance of mathematics has increased rapidly. Even laboratory assistants may need algebra in helping to plan experiments and analyze data, while the professional physiologist will need to understand calculus and probability theory not only to plan and interpret her or his own work, but to comprehend the work of others. If all of these courses are completed in the undergraduate years, the student will have a good background for specializing in physiology in graduate school. The student physiologist also should acquire some knowledge of related biomedical sciences, especially biochemistry and anatomy.

The boundary between physiology and some of the other biosciences is indistinct; indeed, the overlap is so great that an individual trained in one life science sometimes ends up working in another. For example, nobody can tell where physiology lets off and biochemistry begins. Physiology also overlaps with pharmacology, anatomy, genetics, embryology, parasitology, ecology, psychology, and other disciplines. This chapter will describe a few of the related fields.

For more information, contact:

American Physiology Society
9650 Rockville Pike
Bethesda, MD 20814-3991
the-aps.org

Biophysics

Biophysics is one of the newest of the biological sciences, but it has grown rapidly. It is so closely related to physiology that in some schools biophysics and physiology are combined into one department. However, it has become sufficiently independent as a discipline for biophysicists to organize their own society, the Biophysical Society.

The biophysicist's approach to biological problems utilizes the methods of modern physics, higher mathematics, and physical chemistry. The biophysicist addresses some very basic issues, and the findings often have practical consequences. Biophysics has contributed to the study of cancer; to the design of computers, which are analogous in some respects to the brain; and to the development of new drugs. The outstanding advances in biotechnology, genetics, and biomedical engineering were all made possible by the contributions of the biophysicist. Many biological problems cannot be approached without the aid of the instruments and methods of the physical sciences, and even with the physical scientist's point of view.

Many of the reactions within the cells of the body are those involving large and complicated protein molecules, which include reactions in the immune mechanisms, that is, those mechanisms involved in defenses against foreign substances. The biomedical engineer has had some success in prolonging people's lives by replacing failing organs with transplants of healthy ones. These operations are much heralded when they are successful, but there have been instances of disappointment and failure, often because of harmful interactions between the proteins of the transplanted organ and those of the patient receiving the transplant. In other words, the body of the recipient treats the transplant as a foreign and hostile intruder. There has been some success in avoidance of such interactions, but there remains a large problem. Increased knowledge of interactions between proteins offers the most promising approach to the solution of such problems and constitutes an important challenge that future biophysicists can help to meet.

Other interests of biophysicists include the effects of radiation on living matter, the details of the way in which the retina of the eye converts the energy of light into a signal to the brain, and the biological effects of gravity, laser beams, and many others. All interactions of energy with living matter, whether animal or plant, interest the biophysicist. Hence, biophysicists seek to learn how plants convert the energy of sunlight into chemical energy that can be stored in the plant in the form of carbohydrate, which in turn supplies energy to our own bodies.

From this brief description of biophysics, you can see that a biophysicist is a physiologist with a very special approach to physiological problems. The student aiming for a career in biophysics will need an extraordinarily broad base in physics, chemistry, mathematics, and biology, studying these disciplines in high school and continuing them through college and beyond to the doctorate. Some biophysicists recommend as many as ten courses in college mathematics. The student of biophysics will become familiar with the concepts of subjects such as protein chemistry, quantum mechanics, information theory, solid-state physics, and probability theory.

Although the total number of openings for biophysicists may not be as great as for some other disciplines, the high degree of training required limits the number of competitors for the jobs available. Universities employ most biophysicists in teaching and research. Some are employed in space installations and in the armed forces. Large hospitals, laboratories of nonprofit research foundations, and drug companies also make use of the talents of biophysicists.

Biophysics is an intellectually demanding discipline to be undertaken only by those who are willing to work hard and who enjoy mental stimulation. It is a highly experimental field, challenging and exciting, and utilizes the most modern concepts and instruments. If you have the basic motivation for such a study and the capacity to meet the challenge, you will find it a most rewarding vocation.

For more information, contact:

Biophysical Society
9650 Rockville Pike
Bethesda, MD 20814
biophysics.org

Biochemistry

As the name implies, biochemistry is both a biological science and a branch of chemistry. It may be taught in departments of biology, physiology, or chemistry, but many universities have independent departments of biochemistry. While the physiologist may use biochemical techniques to elucidate the function of a tissue or an organ, the biochemist will take special pleasure in studying the chemical processes that occur in active tissues. Both physiology and biochemistry evolved from general biology, but biochemistry could not arise until the advent of organic chemistry.

Considerable progress was made in physiology during the nineteenth century, but it was not until near the close of that century that chemists became aware that all organic substances contain carbon. The chemistry of carbon compounds then became organic chemistry. Biochemistry emerged as a separate discipline when some scientists combined biology and organic chemistry and began to study chemical reactions occurring in living systems. Hence biochemistry is a younger science than physiology and in a sense, may be regarded as the offspring of a marriage between physiology and chemistry. The lineage of biochemistry is apparent in the various names that are sometimes given to it, such as physiological chemistry and biological chemistry.

Biochemists with the highest degrees of education are usually involved in teaching or research, although a growing number may be in administration or in service work. Young people in the early stages of their careers are widely employed as laboratory workers, technicians, or assistants. Many find this type of work to be fully satisfying; advancement as a fully qualified professional research scientist, for example, does not appeal to everyone.

Testing and analytical programs occupy the time of many biochemists, while others work full-time on research and still more are teachers; most teachers in colleges or universities devote part of their time to research. The research may be basic, that is, performed primarily to increase scientific knowledge; or applied, that is, to solve problems with immediate practical application. Many times the research biochemist or the clinical chemist must apply newly discovered techniques to her or his work. This may involve the use of new instruments or new chemical reagents. If existing methods and procedures do not fully meet requirements, the biochemist will need to invent them, test them fully in the laboratory, and then publish the results so that other biochemists may confirm them. In addition to research and teaching, some biochemists, especially in hospital laboratories or in independent testing laboratories, provide services that assist physicians in diagnosing and treating disease. Others, especially those employed by industry, also may aid in quality control.

Colleges of pharmacy, dentistry, medicine, veterinary medicine, and agriculture are among the professional schools that provide opportunities for teaching or research in biochemistry. In these schools, it is not only the departments of biochemistry that employ biochemists; employment also is offered in departments of physiology, pharmacology, microbiology, anatomy, medicine, and others. Departments of biology or chemistry in colleges and universities supply positions for many biochemists.

Hospitals, independent research institutes, public health departments, government laboratories such as the famed National Institutes of Health, and agricultural experiment stations are among those that benefit from the special talents of biochemists. A wide variety of industrial laboratories, including food processors, drug and cosmetic manufacturers, and the huge chemical and petroleum industries, constitute a continuing source of employment opportunities for those interested in applied biochemistry, in basic or applied research, or in scientific administration. Many biochemists, especially clinical chemists, have gone into business for themselves, offering biochemical testing services on a fee or a contract basis. Such testing laboratories may employ biochemists, as well as biochemical laboratory assistants and technicians. The workload of testing laboratories, including those owned and operated by hospitals, has a record of growth; it has been said that the workload doubles approximately every seven years. This, then, constitutes a continually growing demand for those prepared to meet it.

The education a biochemist needs will depend upon what position on the ladder the person wishes to take. For advancement to the top ranks, advanced degrees are desirable, and for the top-notch jobs, only a doctorate will suffice. Training leading to such degrees may usually be obtained while working as a laboratory assistant or teaching fellow. The education of the biochemist need not differ much from that of other specialists in the health sciences, but a good grasp of chemistry, mathematics, and physics is of special importance. Generally speaking, it is not necessary to major in biochemistry during the undergraduate years; most biochemists have majored either in biology or in chemistry, then concentrated on biochemistry in graduate school. Nearly two hundred colleges and universities offer graduate degrees in biochemistry.

Some biochemists have become interested in their specialty after attending medical school and receiving either an M.D. or Ph.D. degree. Biochemists with a medical background usually are employed in medical schools, hospitals, and research laboratories. By whatever route the biochemist enters the profession, he or she will find many opportunities for creative and exciting work.

For more information, contact:

American Society of Biochemistry and Molecular Biology
9650 Rockville Pike
Bethesda, MD 20814-3991
asbmb.org

Pharmacology

Although pharmacology is a basic science that is an important part of the training of all students in all health professions, including pharmacy, medicine, dentistry, and veterinary medicine, the word *pharmacology* is still not understood by many. Only within recent years has there been a move toward offering pharmacology at the undergraduate level in colleges of liberal arts, and the majority of schools do not have such programs. Most medical schools and many pharmacy schools offer courses leading to master's or doctoral degrees in pharmacology. The students who are accepted as candidates in these programs are usually graduates of colleges where they have majored in one of the biological sciences. The biology major should, therefore, become acquainted with the career potential offered by pharmacology. Young people trained in this discipline have had little difficulty getting jobs, even during periods of recession.

To define pharmacology as briefly as possible, it is the study of the interactions of drugs with living systems. By drugs we mean any chemical substances that can be given to a human being or animal that will affect the recipient for good or ill or that will in any way affect the life processes. The living system might be a microscopic part of a cell, an organ of the body, or a whole animal or person, healthy or sick. Physiologists study responses of cells, organs, and organisms, and biochemists study their chemical reactions. Pathologists examine the effects of disease. Pharmacology, then, overlaps with those disciplines and uses their techniques. No one could be a top-notch pharmacologist without a thorough background in physiology and biochemistry.

Physicians and pharmacists also know a great deal about drugs, but to be a physician or a pharmacist is not necessarily to be a pharmacologist. The pharmacologist's knowledge of drugs is unique. The intimate nature of drug action as affected by the size of the dose, method of administration, and solubility in various body fluids; the effects of small changes in the chemical structure of the drug; and the significance of physical properties as related to drug action are among the matters of concern to the pharmacologist but are outside the specific interests of physiologists or biochemists.

Pharmacology is divided into many branches, as are most other life sciences. The general pharmacologist tries to understand the action of a drug in all parts of the body and often is searching for better and safer drugs for treating disease. The interests and methods of comparative pharmacologists might be similar, and their findings might be of interest, for example, to a veterinary physician who needs to treat various species of animals. Molecular pharmacology is more basic in its approach and seeks to discern the interaction between a molecule of a drug and a molecule within a cell of the body. Some of the discoveries of the molecular pharmacologists have given physicians valuable information about, for example, the intimate mechanisms of the nervous system or the actions of the kidneys. Biochemical pharmacologists or biophysical pharmacologists use the techniques of physics and biochemistry; sometimes their primary interest is to determine what the body does to the drug rather than what the drug does to the body. Such information is especially valuable in helping to improve the drugs already available.

Toxicology is a branch of pharmacology specifically concerned with the adverse effects of chemical substances, ranging all the way from minor unwanted effects of useful drugs to the actions of virulent poisons. The toxicologist is equally interested in the immediate effects of a single exposure to a substance and the long-range actions of a drug that a person may need to take daily for many years. Toxicologists are in great demand in the drug industry. No drug is 100 percent safe; one of the duties of the medical or forensic toxicologist is to determine the limits of safety of a drug. Forensic toxicologists are also involved in research into the medical and legal aspects of drug abuse. The industrial toxicologist applies his or her knowledge to the health of workers in industry; a wide variety of industrial concerns utilize such expertise. The environmental toxicologist helps protect public health by studying the effects of water and air pollutants, industrial wastes, household chemicals, food additives, pesticides, and the many other exposures of the modern world.

Some pharmacologists concentrate their studies upon some particular organ or system in the body. For example, the action of drugs upon the nervous system comes under the attention of neuropharmacologists. Their interests are related to those of behavioral pharmacologists who use the techniques of psychology to ascertain the effects of chemical substances upon behavior and psychic functions. These branches of pharmacology have become especially important since the use of drugs that alter behavior has become so widespread.

Deserving of special attention is the clinical pharmacologist who applies the discoveries of other pharmacologists to the human subject and who, of course, also makes many discoveries. Clinical pharmacologists seek to determine whether a particular drug is useful, how it should be used, and what adverse effects it may have. They bridge the gap between the original discovery of a new drug and its use by a practicing physician. Therefore, they must be versed not only in physiology, biochemistry, and pharmacology but in medicine as well. They possess M.D. degrees and sometimes Ph.D.s also. The training of a clinical pharmacologist is a long one, and this specialty is one of the most important and demanding of all the health sciences.

Employment opportunities in pharmacology are available in medical, pharmacy, and veterinary schools, and to an increasing extent in four-year colleges. Pharmacologists are also in demand in government laboratories, especially agencies such as the National Institutes of Health and the Food and Drug Administration. Hospitals and independent nonprofit research laboratories hire many pharmacologists, as do the laboratories of industry, especially the pharmaceutical industry. Several independent laboratories engaged in providing service to other institutions under contract also hire pharmacologists. The variety of activities in which pharmacologists are engaged matches the variety of institutions for which they work.

There are many opportunities for working in a pharmacology laboratory for those without complete professional training, but for the top-level jobs a doctoral degree is essential. During the high school and undergraduate college years, the education of a future pharmacologist parallels that of a physiologist or biochemist. Most helpful will be courses in mathematics through calculus and including statistics; a course in general physics; and chemistry, including organic and physical chemistry. With such a background, whether or not the curriculum includes an undergraduate course in pharmacology, the student will be well equipped to pursue graduate study in most of the basic medical sciences and need not make a final choice among them until graduate school.

For more information, contact:

American Society for Pharmacology and Clinical Therapeutics
9650 Rockville Pike
Bethesda, MD 20814-3995
aspet.org

Nutrition

There are several biosciences concerned with food and nutrition in one way or another. The dietician or nutritionist studies the fate of foodstuffs after digestion and absorption (thus overlapping with physiology and biochemistry) and is especially concerned with the relationship of food to the health and welfare of both the individual and society, and its connection with the cause, treatment, or prevention of disease.

Research is still underway on the nutritional aspects of hypertension, heart ailments, obesity, tooth decay, and possibly even arthritis and cancer. Some unfortunate children are born with errors in the metabolism of foodstuffs that lead to mental retardation and early death; an example of this is the disease known as phenylketonuria. Largely because of the efforts of nutritionists, many of these children have been able to develop in a nearly normal fashion, and research is continuing.

Some nutritional discoveries have far-reaching results. Not so long ago a diagnosis of pernicious anemia was almost the same as a death warrant. With the discovery of vitamin B_{12}, the means for treating this disease was at hand. But B_{12} was to have an unexpected and quite unrelated significance in nutrition, for it proved to be a factor that increased the efficiency with which meat animals converted hay and grain into body-building protein.

There are several types of careers related to nutrition. Research dieticians are scientists contributing new knowledge on subjects such as human or animal metabolism, the interrelationships of foods, and the effects of nutrients on health. They are employed in universities; in medical, dental, veterinary, and agricultural colleges; in government agencies; in international agencies; and in industry, especially industrial concerns engaged in supplying dietary supplements for either human or animal use. Some research dieticians work for food manufacturers or grocery store chains, analyzing the nutritional content of food for labeling purposes or for marketing. Community dieticians apply the science of nutrition in various fields of health care and are primarily employed by home health agencies, health maintenance organizations (HMOs), and human service agencies. Administrative dieticians apply the principles of nutrition in the planning and management of food-service programs in hospitals, schools, and other institutions. Clinical dieticians prescribe diets, select foods, and counsel hospitals, clinics, nursing homes, and other individuals or communities.

The wide range of different kinds of jobs in nutrition is reflected in the range of educational requirements. The American Dietetic Association maintains a list of colleges that provide training courses for high school graduates to qualify as dietetic assistants or dietetic technicians; these courses may lead to an associate degree. There are also undergraduate programs leading to a baccalaureate degree as a dietician; other graduates may become approved dieticians after a suitable internship. In many states, there are universities that also offer advanced training to the master's and doctoral levels. The education and training of the research dietician is comparable to that of other bioscientists. Physiology, microbiology, organic chemistry, and biochemistry are essential. Mathematics, statistics, computer science, psychology, sociology, and economics should not be neglected. As in all sciences, the research nutritionist with a doctoral degree has an advantage.

For more information, contact:

American Dietetic Association
120 South Riverside Plaza, Suite 2000
Chicago, IL 60606-6995
eatright.org

Immunology

Immunology is the study of the way in which the body protects itself against a foreign invader, whether it is a substance producing an allergic reaction, an invasion by a disease-producing microbe, an organ transplant, a parasite, or a virus. The reaction of the body to each of these insults is called an immune response. Each immune response is very specific; that is, each particular kind of invader produces an immune response that is specifically directed toward that invading material. The invading stimulus is a chemical substance (called an antigen) and the body produces another chemical substance (antibody) that reacts chemically with it. Hence, immunology could be considered from one point of view to be a branch of biochemistry. Since the immune system is one of the normally functioning systems of the body, immunology is also a branch of physiology. Since an immune response is often a part of a disease process, immunology is to some degree a part of the science of pathology. Since immune responses sometimes have to be treated by physicians, immunology is also a part of medicine.

Diseases caused by bacteria and viruses are not the only things that excite the interest of immunologists. If you suffer from hay fever, if you have symptoms like a common cold when you breathe house dust or animal danders, if you have a severe rash after contact with poison ivy, if insect stings cause severe reactions, then you are experiencing an immune response that, instead of protecting you, is causing you distress. Some people even develop such responses to some of their own cells or tissues—these are called autoimmune disease; perhaps the most common of these is rheumatoid arthritis, which makes millions of people suffer. All of these furnish challenges to the immunologist, who seeks knowledge that will enable physicians to alleviate the symptoms of such diseases and, in the end, cure or prevent them.

Other challenges for the future of immunology include the control of adverse reactions in blood transfusions and in the transplantation of tissues and organs. Especially exciting are the prospects for possible immunological treatment of cancer, for the selective removal from the blood of troublesome substances that trigger immune responses, or for reducing the risks from those responses that are inherited. Finding a cure for the deadly disease AIDS also presents a challenge for immunologists. No wonder that the National Institute of Allergy and Infectious Diseases of the National Institutes of Health has referred to immunology as "a discipline whose time has come."

Immunology presents career opportunities ranging all the way from laboratory assistants and technicians to professional scientists in charge of large laboratories. At all levels, the work is of absorbing interest and gives great personal satisfaction. The worker in immunology uses many of the laboratory techniques of biochemistry and microbiology. The better the person's preparation in these fields, the better he or she will be able to perform the duties, and the greater pleasure the worker will derive from the daily activities. For full professional standing and the best-rated jobs, the undergraduate preparation should be about the same as that described for the other biomedical sciences. This includes a grasp of biology, including microbiology, with chemistry through organic and preferably physical chemistry; a course in physics; some knowledge of computer science; and, of course, a basic understanding of mathematics.

Immunologists employed by educational institutions divide their time between teaching and research; this includes more than half of all members of the profession. Training in immunology may be obtained in almost any university having a medical school, and there are a few immunologists in departments of biology. There are relatively few departments of immunology; most often it is a section within a department. Departments of microbiology, biochemistry, and medicine most frequently employ immunologists. A few hospitals and research foundations also give employment to immunologists, but the leading employer outside the medical schools is the federal government, especially the National Institutes of Health. There are also some openings in laboratories supported by local and state governments. No discipline surpasses immunology in opportunities on the frontier of science.

For more information, contact:

American Association of Immunologists
9650 Rockville Pike
Bethesda, MD 20814-3995
aai.org

Pathology

Pathology is both a basic biomedical science and a specialty of medicine. By the use of the techniques of biology, chemistry, and physics, pathologists examine the tissues and fluids of the body. They seek to determine the presence of any measurable or visible changes produced by disease or by any other interference with normal bodily structure or function. Their findings enable them to judge whether a given specimen has come from a healthy individual or if there is disease or injury. The nature of a disease and the effectiveness of treatment may also be revealed.

Pathology, then, is a link between the basic biomedical sciences and clinical medicine. Most pathologists are physicians who have specialized in this particular field. Medicine and its specialties are beyond the scope of this book; we are interested in pathology as a biological science. In fact, there is a demand for pathologists who are not physicians. They include dental and veterinary pathologists as well as a growing number of individuals in research and service jobs who have a Ph.D. in pathology. Indeed many of the members of the American Society for Experimental Pathology have advanced work in areas other than that for the M.D. degree.

In addition to the top-grade professional jobs, there is a demand for workers in pathology laboratories, especially those trained for the many demanding technical jobs. Physicians are placing more and more reliance on the findings of the laboratory to assist them in diagnosing disease and in following the progress of therapy. Some of the laboratory jobs also give an opportunity for the young worker to study for the most advanced professional qualifications.

Some diseases, such as diabetes and leukemia, can be identified only through laboratory methods. The pathologist is essential for the diagnosis of such diseases and supplies the means for following responses of the patient to treatment. For supervising a laboratory bearing such important responsibilities, a pathologist should qualify for a special certificate from the American Board of Pathology. In most cases, the pathologist also will be a teacher, aiding in the training of medical students, nurses, interns, medical technologists, and resident physicians.

Teaching, research, and service—these are the outlets for the pathologist's skills. Nearly every accredited hospital employs pathologists. A pathology department is a prominent feature in medical schools; dental and veterinary schools also have such departments. Some pathologists operate independent laboratories that provide service to physicians in private practice. Independent research institutions operated by nonprofit foundations employ many pathologists and pathology technologists. A particularly important source of employment opportunities is the federal government, as well as state and local public health installations. The armed services operate large institutes for research and service in pathology, and the National Institutes of Health and the Food and Drug Administration have particular need for those with skills in pathology.

Laboratories concerned with studies on the safety of drugs provide a large and expanding demand. Individuals with Ph.D. degrees in pathology, or with training in veterinary pathology, are especially in demand in these establishments. Studies on the safety of new drugs must be conducted at length and with great skill on experimental animals before the drug can be tried on human beings. After the animals have received the new drug, the fluids and tissues of their bodies must be subjected to the same tests as those made on human patients in disease. In fact, no patient ever gets quite as thorough an examination as do these animals. Federal laws and regulations make such studies mandatory, and the standards are constantly being elevated; hence the demand for personnel is very great.

The tests just described are performed in the laboratories of drug manufacturers and in many laboratories operated by the government, such as the National Institutes of Health and the Food and Drug Administration. In addition, many independent laboratories carry out similar studies. Several commercial pathology laboratories perform such tests for others on a contract basis.

For more information, contact:

American Society for Investigational Pathology
9650 Rockville Pike
Bethesda, MD 20814-3995
asip.org

Clinical Medicine

Medicine is one of the oldest branches of science, and today medicine not only is one of the most technologically advanced of all the biosciences, it is also one of the most diverse. Doctors can choose to concentrate their practices in a primary care setting, specialize in one very technical area such as eye surgery, or offer a combination of skills. In addition to maintaining a clinical practice, many are affiliated with academic health centers where they enjoy teaching and doing research. Whether they may choose to work with children or adults, the rewarding, long-term relationships with their patients is what makes many biology majors choose medicine as a career.

Medicine, like most health care professions, has become an industry. Twenty years ago, doctors were secure in their role as the most expert of the health care providers. They were the only practitioners who were closely allied with hospitals. In today's competitive environment, doctors are faced with competition from their former referral sources. Although they are still among the highest paid health care professionals, income has become a variable factor in a changing workplace and the cost of running a practice, including malpractice insurance premiums, has increased dramatically. As start-up costs increase, few young physicians see much future in going out on their own. Getting started now is likely to mean a less independent approach like:

- Buying an established practice
- Entering into an arrangement with a hospital
- Responding to recruiting by a rural community
- Sharing at least some facilities and functions with another colleague
- Cooperating with a number of other physicians in a "clinic without walls"

Pessimistic health care industry analysts predict that solo practice will be restricted to small towns and underserved areas. Rather than face the austerity of the start-up years, many young doctors will contract with hospitals and HMOs. Physicians in California and New Mexico have come up with solutions they think will help solo physicians and small group practices remain viable and independent. In both locations, physicians have formed their own corporations that provide a wide range of business services for doctors who want to remain in their own offices. The corporations pool expenses and achieve savings on purchases of equipment, medical supplies, bookkeeping, accounting services, health insurance premiums, and pension administration. Some groups even share office space, a receptionist, and medical technicians. In this "clinic without walls" scenario, a new doctor could share the overhead of starting a practice with physicians in other specialties or with other doctors. Although starting a private practice is risky, most doctors still believe that the personal freedom it affords makes it all worthwhile.

Doctors are the mostly highly educated of the health care professionals. They are expected to continue their education throughout their careers. To qualify for entry into an approved medicine residency program, an applicant must have either a Medical Doctor (M.D.) or a Doctor of Osteopathy (D.O.) degree and have completed one year of post-graduate training known as an internship or PGY 1. The internship is usually not in medicine, but in internal medicine, surgery, pediatrics, or a number of other disciplines. The competition for medicine residency positions is intense. Applicants interview at many institutions hoping to be accepted at their first choice. In mid-March, residents and programs participate in a computerized match administered by the National Resident Matching Program, which provides an impartial venue for the pairing of residents with programs. After the match, the residents receive contracts from the programs outlining the conditions of their employment and training.

Residency training is one of the most rigorous parts of the training. The resident must see a large number and variety of patients to gain the experience needed for practice and board certification. It is often necessary for residents to rotate through several hospitals to meet these requirements. The resident's educational experience must be designed and supervised by the teaching program director. In the past, this training was described in terms of the hours and types of experiences. Today, residents must demonstrate that they have mastered certain competencies. These include:

- Patient care that is compassionate, appropriate, and effective for the treatment of health problems and the promotion of health

- Medical knowledge about established and evolving biomedical, clinical, and cognate (that is, epidemiological and social-behavioral) sciences and the application of this knowledge to patient care
- Practice-based learning and improvement that involves investigation and evaluation of their own patient care, appraisal and assimilation of scientific evidence, and improvements in patient care
- Interpersonal and communication skills that result in effective information exchange and teaming with patients and their families

These competencies are developed over a three-year period by combining classroom instruction with supervised hands-on experience, called clinical training. As the resident progresses, he or she becomes more independent in patient care responsibilities and takes on increasing responsibility for teaching and supervising more junior residents. In all types of residency training, including medicine, the program director and the physicians on the faculty are responsible for ensuring that residents are progressing competently in their education and that they in no way endanger the patients who are involved in their clinical experiences. The work hours for residents are long when compared to other professions. However, for the health of the residents and the safety of their patients, their schedules are monitored to ensure that they do not spend more than eighty hours per week in patient care duties. Fellowships are for doctors who want to continue their education beyond residency to become experts in a subspecialty. Their hands-on training is generally focused on a particular type of patient or disease. They train at larger medical centers where they are expected to participate in research projects, publish papers, and present at conferences in addition to caring for patients.

The distinction between board certification and licensing is often confusing. All practicing physicians, including doctors, must be licensed in the states where they see patients. Board certification is a voluntary credential; it shows the attainment of the highest level of knowledge and skills in the field of medicine.

The purpose of the examinations given to doctors for board certification is to determine whether they have the knowledge, skills, and experience to provide patient care according to the high standards set by their profession. The American Board of Medicine administers both oral and written examinations. Passing the examinations means that the doctor is board certified, a distinction all well-informed patients and referring physicians look for when choosing a specialist for their patients. Board certification is good for ten years, at which time a doctor must present proof of participation in continuing education programs and be in good standing with his or her state licensing board.

Every state in the United States has a medical licensing board that reviews the applications of health practitioners who would like to provide patient care within its jurisdiction. A doctor who has completed his or her residency and who is board certified or eligible to take the boards must fill out an application that is submitted to the licensing board. All of the information, including medical school attendance, residency training, and references from hospitals and other doctors, is checked by the state licensing board. It also queries the National Practitioner Databank, which is a federally mandated program that compiles information on physicians who have had problems such as hospital suspensions, revoked licenses in other states, excessive malpractice cases, or other issues with the quality of care provided to their patients. When all of the information is verified as correct and the physician is deemed qualified to practice in the state, a license is issued and must be renewed on a regular basis. Doctors, like other physicians, must show that they have participated in the amount of continuing education that is required by the state for relicensing. For doctors, education is a lifelong pursuit.

Recent statistics from the American Medical Association showed that medicine is still a popular choice among physicians. In the AMA's data on the distribution of physicians in thirty-six recognized specialties, medicine was listed as the thirteenth largest group of doctors. Among the nine surgical subspecialties, medicine ranked third behind general surgery and orthopedics. There are currently about fifteen thousand doctors in the United States.

The average income of a doctor currently ranges from about $165,000 to $223,000, based on a number of variables including location and the size and maturity of the practice. After years of steady gain in both income and growth in numbers, some experts believe that the medicine market has peaked. Medicare reimbursement has been reduced several times in the past few years. Private insurers and HMOs, following Medicare's lead, have reduced reimbursement to doctors as well. In addition to reductions in income, doctors have also had tremendous increases in expenses, particularly in the area of malpractice insurance.

The demand for doctors is expected to increase as the population ages. Demand will be greatest in rural and typically underserved areas. Other trends that will negatively impact the demand for doctors are the recent technological advances that have eliminated the need for surgery, and in many states, the scope of practice for other practitioners like optometrists has broadened to overlap that of their M.D. colleagues. Patients who are insured through managed-care plans are also sometimes denied access to specialists unless referred by their primary care physician, who is encouraged by the insurance plans to perform basic health care.

On the supply side, there are fewer new graduates and, although there is the tendency among many older physicians to work beyond traditional retirement age, doctors, like surgeons, lose their dexterity as they age. In short, if new doctors are flexible about where they work, they can do very well.

For more information, contact:

American Medical Association
515 North State Street
Chicago, IL 60610
ama-assn.org

6

CAREERS IN BIOTECHNOLOGY

BIOTECHNOLOGY USED TO be known as the applied biosciences because it used the discoveries of the pure sciences, discussed in the last chapter, to apply new solutions to the practical problems of everyday life. Biotechnology uses cells—the building blocks of life—and cellular processes to create new or improved products such as pharmaceuticals. This is not a new science. As soon as early man discovered that he could breed domesticated animals and improve the production of crops by cross-pollinating plants, biotechnology was invented. Even before we knew the pure scientific reason for these innovations, we engaged in biotechnological research.

This chapter reviews several of the biotechnologies because they are many and they are growing. This is the area of the biosciences where job opportunities are the most numerous and lucrative. If you are in high school now, there will be new biotechnical careers available to you that are unheard of today. Most people will think of the pharmaceutical industry when you mention biotechnology, but this is a much more diverse industry. Here are some statistics and facts provided by the Biotechnology Industry Organization (BIO):

- There are 1,457 biotechnology companies in the United States, of which 342 are publicly held.
- The biotechnology industry has mushroomed since 1992, with revenues increasing from $8 billion in 1992 to $34.8 billion in 2001.
- The U.S. biotechnology industry currently employs 191,000 people; that's more than all the people employed by the toy and sporting goods industries.
- Biotechnology is one of the most research-intensive industries in the world. The U.S biotech industry spent $15.7 billion on research and development in 2001.
- The top five biotech companies spent an average of $133,600 per employee on research and development in 2001.
- The Food and Drug Administration (FDA), the Environmental Protection Agency (EPA), and the Department of Agriculture (USDA) regulate the biotech industry.

According to BIO, here are some of the more recent accomplishments of the biotechnological community, which show the diversity in the problems it solves:

- There are more than 370 biotech drug products and vaccines currently in clinical trials targeting more than 200 diseases, including various cancers, Alzheimer's disease, heart disease, diabetes, multiple sclerosis, AIDS, and arthritis.

- Biotechnology is responsible for hundreds of medical diagnostic tests that keep the blood supply safe from the AIDS virus and detect other conditions early enough to be successfully treated. Home pregnancy tests are also biotechnology diagnostic products.
- Consumers already are enjoying biotechnology foods such as papaya, soybeans, and corn. Hundreds of biopesticides and other agricultural products are being used to improve our food supply and to reduce our dependence on conventional chemical pesticides.
- Environmental biotechnology products make it possible to clean up hazardous waste more efficiently by harnessing pollution-eating microbes without the use of caustic chemicals.
- Industrial biotechnology applications have led to cleaner processes that produce less waste and use less energy and water in such industrial sectors as chemicals, pulp and paper, textiles, food, energy, and metals and minerals. For example, most laundry detergents produced in the United States contain biotechnology-based enzymes.
- DNA fingerprinting, a biotech process, has dramatically improved criminal investigation and forensic medicine, as well as afforded significant advances in anthropology and wildlife management.

The biotechnology industry has many types of jobs. Some of these jobs are discussed in Chapter 7 and have a lot to do with the business side of the biotech world. There are also many career options on the manufacturing side, where the actual production of biotech goods is accomplished. But, as we have seen, many resources are committed to research. This is the area of the biotechnologies where the work of scientists is indispensable. If you like the idea of exploring a side of biology that will result in a tangible, beneficial product, then this is the type of research for you.

How do you keep up with where the latest jobs are in the biotech industry? Watch the news—both science and financial—monitor the website listed below, join a biotech association, find a mentor who is working in this field. If you choose biotech as your career path, you may be creating your own job.

For more information, contact:

Biotechnical Industry Organization (BIO)
1225 Eye Street NW, Suite 400
Washington, D.C. 20005
(202) 962-9200
bio.org

Pharmaceuticals

The process of discovering new drugs and bringing them to consumers is a huge undertaking. This is made possible by a complex group of research laboratories and manufacturing businesses known as the pharmaceutical industry. There are about twenty-five hundred pharmaceutical employers in the United States who provided more than 315,000 jobs in the year 2000. According the Bureau of Labor, salaries of pharmaceutical company workers are higher than those in other types of manufacturing, and half of the workers hold college degrees, which reflects the industry's investment in research and development activities. Since the drug manufacturing process involves basic bench research through marketing of FDA-approved medications, many of the jobs in this industry are discussed elsewhere in this book. Here are a few of them:

Basic and applied
research
Biological research
Bacteriology
Microbiology
Biochemistry
Pharmacology
Zoology
Virology
Botany
Pathology
Toxicology
Medical research
Biomedical engineering
Medical monitoring
Drug safety surveillance
Data management
(bioinformatics)
Scientific writing

Manufacturing
production
Auditors and monitors
Clinical laboratory
testing
Sales and marketing
Technology transfer
Policy analysis
Information services
Financial advising
Clinical research
monitoring
Computer programming
Biostatistics
Quality control and
assurance
Patent and regulatory
law

About 22 percent of the jobs in the pharmaceutical industry are in professional occupations, namely for scientists and technologists. Needless to say, a job with a pharmaceutical company is a good first choice. There are many opportunities to expand your knowledge and skills, find a mentor, and move up the ladder.

For more information, contact:

American Association of Pharmaceutical Scientists
1650 King Street
Alexandria, VA 22314-2747
(703) 548-3000
aaps.org

Bioinformatics

If you like computers and biology, this is the career choice for you. The purpose of this job is to gather, store, retrieve, and manipulate data according to needs of computer users. There is a tremendous amount of data that is generated by research worldwide, especially from huge projects such as the human genome project. In fact, the history of the modern field of study called bioinformatics really began when the genome project coincided with the information revolution. Before that there was the field of computational biology, which dealt mainly with the analysis of data. The title of computational biologist is often used interchangeably with bioinformatist or bioinformatician. However, a bioinformatics specialist is also trained in the gathering, organization, and retrieval of data, as well as data analysis. There are other variations of the job title, which shows how new this field is.

Whatever you call it, there is a tremendous need for people versed in science and computers. In the biomedical sciences, bioinformatics specialists computerize data from clinical drug trials and automate patient records in hospitals. Bioinformatics is a growing field, but the best jobs are in the biotech industry, especially in pharmaceutical companies. The competition for these jobs can be challenging. However, you will find that bioinformatics is an integral part of all of the branches of biology that we examine in this book, and there is such a growing need for informatics that several universities have developed crossover programs for scientists to become more computer literate. Large data processing companies, such as IBM, have started divisions to provide computational services to research and biotech firms. Special computer skills, such as the ability to perform biosimulations, which are computerized projections or predictive models, is one of the most sought-after skills in the biotech industry today. A skilled bioinformatics specialist can command a six-figure starting salary wherever he or she goes, which far exceeds the beginning range of most new life scientists.

While many bioinformation experts work with databanks of carefully guarded corporate secrets, there are some who have developed the National Biological Information Infrastructure, a government sponsored database that anyone can access for current information on the biosciences. The data service (nbii.gov) was started in the mid-1990s and has many resources such as links to science news, curricula for teachers, and a search engine that directs users to documents and data sources on any biosciences subject. It's a mini-Internet of biological information! Try it.

How do you prepare for a career in informatics? Insiders advise that you take a course in computational biology and familiarize yourself with Web languages, a variety of operating systems, and relational databases, for example, UNIX, PERL, HTML, C++, and SQL. If you like computers, you know that there are lots of books on software. Also, some programming skills are necessary, but one does not need great expertise. It is a challenging field because you need to stay current with changes in both biology and computer science. This is one of those careers where your technical experience will outweigh your education. Some bioinformatists are M.D.s or Ph.D.s, but an advanced degree is not necessary.

For more information, contact bioplanet.com.

Genomics

You probably know what a gene is, but do you know the definition of a genome? It is bigger than a gene. In fact, it is the set of chromosomes in each living organism that contains all of its genes and related DNA. The study of genomes is called genomics, and in genomics there are two branches: structural genomics involves genome mapping or sequencing; functional genomics is concerned with the roles that genes play and how they function as a biological system.

Genome mapping seems like a daunting task. There are so many complex organisms in the world. But, in fact, most living things have many genomes in common. Mapping them helps to distinguish similar members of a species from each other, like DNA identification. The genetic maps of humans and chimpanzees, for instance, are different by only 1 percent.

In the past, agricultural crops and livestock had to be bred and grown to maturity to determine their uniquely inherited traits. Today, with gene mapping, this can be done with highly sophisticated electronic equipment in a very short time.

For more information, contact:

National Human Genome Research Institute
National Institutes of Health
9000 Rockville Pike
Bethesda, MD 20892-2152
(301) 402-0911
genome.gov

Biomedical Engineering

The biomedical engineer finds the answers to problems in patient care and clinical research using his or her training and experience in biology, medicine, and engineering. The results of the biomedical engineers' work are usually devices or techniques that involve mechanical means of operation. However, they can be as small as a computer chip that functions as an implantable drug pump, or as large as a magnetic resonance imager, which when mounted on a tractor trailer truck can provide diagnostic services in the most remote locations.

Many exciting advances are being made in improvements in the care and rehabilitation of people who are handicapped by the malfunction of some body organ. Such organs can be supported or even replaced by other organs or devices. Some of the more spectacular achievements in this field—for example, a completely artificial heart—capture the public's imagination and obtain much publicity. As interesting as such advances are, they actually represent only the tip of the iceberg of applications of new technologies to human problems. Biomedical engineering is really a combination of medicine and engineering technology, and it is changing at such a rate that it is difficult to predict exactly what the career opportunities may be in the early part of the twenty-first century.

Some applications of advances in physics and engineering to biological and medical problems have been in use for several years; these include implanted pacemakers for the heart, which are devices that generate electrical impulses to initiate heartbeats when the heart's own pacemaker falters. Artificial kidneys in the form of dialysis machines are prolonging many lives, but future technology will greatly improve and simplify the use of such devices. Advances are being made in the replacement of limbs by prostheses that respond to the body's own neuromuscular impulses. Visualization of internal organs without the intervention of x-rays is also becoming possible through the use of ultrasound, nuclear magnetic resonance (NMR), and computed tomography (CT) technology. At a still more sophisticated stage are research efforts toward development of artificial sense organs, including even eyes.

The number of career opportunities available in biomedical engineering expands as research develops new applications of these technologies.

For more information, contact:

American College of Clinical Engineering
5200 Butler Pike
Plymouth Meeting, PA 19462-1298
(610) 825-6067
accenet.org

Agricultural Sciences

The application of biological and physical sciences to the production of food and fiber forms the very foundation of the success of our civilization. It has helped to make American output levels the envy of the world. It is no wonder, then, that an extraordinarily large and varied number of careers can be found in these fields. The *Occupational Outlook Handbook* of the Bureau of Labor Statistics, U.S. Department of Labor, groups agricultural scientists, like biological scientists, in the category of life scientists. It estimated that in the mid- to late 1990s, agricultural scientists held more than twenty-five thousand jobs. An additional eighteen thousand people were employed in agricultural science faculty positions in colleges and universities.

Agricultural scientists come from a wide variety of training programs and engage in many different kinds of work. Some of them have already been discussed; such disciplines as plant pathology, entomology, ecology, fisheries biology, and genetics are among those described in previous chapters that have applications here.

Examples of agricultural sciences that may be regarded as applied biology include agronomy, which applies biological science to such practices as crop breeding and production; the testing of new varieties of plants; and plant propagation. Horticulture is a related field, embracing not only the breeding and culture of plants, but problems in their storage and handling. Ornamental as well as food plants are considered. Forestry is a related discipline; it is discussed later in this chapter.

Animal husbandry is an agricultural science concerned with the breeding, nutrition, and overall quality of livestock. Poultry science and dairy science are sometimes considered as separate branches of animal husbandry.

Soil scientists are interested in the biological effects of soils as affected by physical, chemical, and other properties. Food technology applies science to the production, processing, preparation, and distribution of food. For example, such familiar items as freeze-dried coffee, frozen orange juice concentrate, and dehydrated vegetables are the results of the efforts of food technologists—as are the packaging innovations that permit them to be marketed. The food technologist must know something of nutrition, physiology, biochemistry, microbiology, and related sciences.

A highly developed specialty is that of seed technologist. Seed technology, a surprisingly wide-ranging field, has a place for people trained in botany, genetics, agronomy, entomology, and several other specialties. The seed technologist and seed analyst may supervise harvesting procedures of seeds, conduct tests for purity and germination, evaluate storage procedures, devise methods for control of insects and fungal infestations, and perform many other procedures. Research in the field may be concerned with breeding improved varieties, increasing seed yield, and improving processes involved in the handling and distribution of seeds. Special problems and opportunities may be presented by the introduction of new varieties resulting from genetic research, and the seed technologist keeps abreast of these developments.

It has been estimated that there are about 350,000 species of plants capable of converting solar energy, carbon dioxide from the air, and water into complex organic substances that form the basis of the food chain. Some 10,000 of these fit somewhere into the scheme of human economic activity, including about 3,000 that have been grown for food. Only a few of these, however, are of major commercial importance—one hundred species or so—and only about fifteen fill the bulk of the food requirements of our species. It is apparent that much remains to be discovered about many thousands of kinds of plants that could possibly be utilized.

Individuals trained in the sciences related to agriculture, horticulture, and aquaculture have many career opportunities in addition to research. For example, one of the nation's largest industries is the production of livestock for meat. There are managerial and production jobs in this industry that benefit from the knowledge of physiology, nutrition, genetics, and range management that the bioscientist provides. Skills in engineering and business management will add to the value of the person seeking such jobs. Animal and plant products also undergo further processing before being offered to the consumer, and processing plants employ many thousands of trained people. Careers also exist in the communications aspect of agribusiness. Such careers require, in addition to technical competence, facilities in writing or public speaking. A thorough knowledge of English is a valuable asset for any career, but it is especially necessary for the many jobs available in trade publications, livestock magazines, advertising agencies, and many other agencies servicing the industry. Individuals trained in animal science advise food processors, act as consultants to engineers who design machinery and equipment used in agriculture, assist breeders of horses, are involved in the breeding and maintenance of laboratory animals, and help in the production and testing of chemical products for use in animal or human nutrition or medicine—to mention just a few applications of their skills.

The land-grant colleges located in each state, as well as many other colleges, including some community colleges, offer training in animal science or other science applicable within the context of the above discussion. A typical course includes, in addition to the basic foundation in humanities and biological and physical sciences, applied subjects such as animal breeding, reproduction, nutrition, and various aspects of managing and handling animals. Many programs also offer a number of support courses in areas such as food science, forage production and use, crop production, and soil science. In addition, communication skills and the economics of agribusiness may be covered, including computer science. The learning is not all from books, for most such schools maintain flocks of poultry, herds of livestock, dairies, and even facilities for practicing the production and packaging of foodstuffs and other products. Practice also is afforded in the all-important paperwork. These specialty courses, of course, come after one has obtained the sort of background that any well-educated person should have in basic science, mathematics, languages, and the humanities.

After obtaining such training, employment opportunities may be sought in many areas, including some of the industries mentioned above. Private research foundations employ many scientists with training in applied biology, as do industries engaged in service to agriculture, food processing, and forestry products. The agricultural scientist may work in the classroom, laboratory, or experiment station. Agricultural colleges employ many teachers and research workers in biology. To fill such jobs, the student will generally need education beyond the baccalaureate degree, and many of the colleges offer graduate work leading to advanced degrees. Research agencies of the federal government and state agricultural experiment stations employ many thousands of agricultural scientists. Those in charge of the various projects typically have doctoral degrees, but there are many rewarding jobs that can be filled by those with baccalaureate or master's degrees. The person wishing eventually to obtain a doctorate often can fill the junior positions on the staff while working for a more advanced degree.

For more information, contact:

Agricultural Research Services
ars.usda.gov

Forestry

Like agricultural science, forestry is a highly practical subject. Indeed, in some lists, forestry is classified with the agricultural sciences. A forester must have training in both the scientific and practical aspects of the management of forestlands. Timber is an important biological resource, and it is the forester's job to see that it not only is used but also is perpetually maintained.

Foresters, like plant pathologists, are concerned about plant diseases. Like entomologists, they must be familiar with insects and their effects, and like ecologists, they must understand the whole of the forest environment and be interested in conservation and the management of wildlife. Foresters must have some expertise in all those fields. In addition, some foresters must learn how to manage outdoor recreation areas. An understanding of many of the technical aspects of wood products, pulp, and paper is also important.

Much of the forester's work is outdoors, but there is a great deal more to it than a perpetual outdoor hiking trip: much of the work is arduous and hazardous. As the forester gains experience, there may be more administrative work and less fieldwork to do.

A bachelor's degree in forestry is the minimum educational requirement for a career in forestry, and many employers prefer graduates with advanced degrees. Curricula stress liberal arts, communication skills, and computer science in addition to technical forestry subjects. Many colleges require students to complete a field session in a camp operated by the college. There are about fifty-five colleges in the United States offering courses leading to a bachelor's or higher degree in forestry. Most such programs are accredited by the Society of American Foresters.

To give some idea of the variety of jobs available to one trained in forestry, consider this partial list: lumber inspector, forest ecologist, forest products technologist, wood products salesperson, forestry information specialist, campground supervisor, forest pathologist, urban forester, Christmas tree grower, wood fuel expert, tree geneticist, forest pest controller, forest consultant, and tree service expert.

Although the federal government is the largest employer of foresters, many states, cities, universities, and private corporations also offer employment opportunities. Private employers include lumber, pulp, paper, and other manufacturers of wood products, as well as railroads, electric utilities, water companies, recreation clubs, and owners of large private estates. Several departments and bureaus of the federal government employ foresters, but the majority of such employees are in the U.S. Forest Service.

For more information, contact:

USDA Forest Service
fs.fed.us

7

NONTRADITIONAL CAREERS IN THE BIOLOGICAL SCIENCES

IN HER BOOK *Nontraditional Careers in Science*, Karen Kreeger Young, a marine biologist turned science writer, defines a nontraditional career as a "nonresearch position, but one in which a scientifically trained person still uses the skills, knowledge and expertise learned in graduate school." The advice given by the author and the many nontraditional scientists that she interviewed was to follow your heart in selecting this type of career. The career options that are discussed in this chapter are just a few of the ways in which a love of science can be combined with another interest.

In general, these career opportunities:

- Are rapidly expanding because of reduced government funding of research and the need for scientists to find work outside the university laboratory or to act as liaisons between private sector business and nonprofit laboratories
- Are open to candidates with less than a Ph.D. degree

- Are sometimes irreversible; you cannot go back to the lab if you make a transition
- Require you to take an entry-level job or internship to break into a new field
- Begin with informational interviewing of experts in the field, who then form a new network of job contacts
- Reduce your income temporarily, but provide more earning potential
- Require a "retooling" of your scientist's résumé to reflect experience in your new field, even if it was volunteer work.
- Available to people who network, so join local chapters of professional associations in your new field

Educating Children and Nonscientists

There is no doubt that people today need to know more about biology. It is part of their daily lives and a better grasp of the facts would make decisions easier. Who better than biologists to educate us? Many biologists teach. But most teach at a college or university. For those who believe that the general public, not just college students, should be more bioliterate, there are several strategies. The first is to start young, that is, to teach in elementary and secondary schools. The second is through informal instruction at public science venues such as museums and zoos. Either way, general skills include being able to explain science to nonscientists. The advantage you gain is the gratification of making a contribution to your local community.

Today, there are about nine thousand biology teachers in the United States and Canada. Biologists who choose to work with young children instead of college-level students value the year-long relationship with their students and feel good about the long-term effects of being a mentor. When graduating students choose biology as a college major and career goal, it is the ultimate compliment. Of course, being a teacher requires a desire to work with children and, in most places, a teaching certificate including student teaching is mandatory. However, for new teachers, a bachelor's degree or B.S. is sufficient to start. In fact, in some school districts science teachers are so scarce that emergency certification is granted; formal certification can be attained while the teacher is being paid to work. This is one career where a Ph.D. in biology is not required, although some teachers who want to become school administrators do pursue a doctoral degree in education. Some biologists who have made this transition will tell you that teaching requires a different type of patience than that necessary to do lab work. It also requires creativity, flexibility, understanding, and good planning skills. To try out teaching as a profession and to prepare for this career, work as a tutor or lead a youth group; then enroll in education courses at a local university.

For those who are interested in teaching outside the formal classroom, there are opportunities for instructing visitors to museums, zoos, and aquariums. Some of these educators also provide special instruction to science teachers or serve as resource persons for other groups or organizations. Biologists who are looking for their first job in informal science will find that there is a lot of competition. It is hard to get a position unless you have experience. Volunteering at a museum is a good way to get experience.

The training for informal education is mainly hands-on and usually does not require a Ph.D. However, sometimes a Ph.D. is an advantage, particularly if the institution is supported by outside funding. Foundations and government agencies believe that an expert gives credibility to an educational program. When you work for a museum or science center, your duties can extend beyond education, particularly if you are the only scientist on the staff. These duties can include supervising staff, seeking grant monies, educating the public, designing and maintaining (sometimes building) exhibits, writing educational materials, or producing media or interactive elements for exhibits. Since most employers are nonprofit organizations, the salaries are often lower than those for laboratory jobs; but the work is creative, you have a lot of autonomy, and it is usually very enjoyable. It is best to start your job hunting by contacting a local museum or science center.

For more information, contact:

National Association of Biology Teachers
11250 Roger Bacon Drive, #19
Reston, VA 20190-5202
nabt.org
(800) 406-0775

National Science Teachers Association
1840 Wilson Boulevard
Arlington, VA 22201
nsta.org
(703) 243-7100

Association of Science-Technology Centers (ASTC)
1025 Vermont Avenue NW, Suite 500
Washington, D.C. 20005-3516
astc.org
(202) 783-7200

American Association of Museums (AAM)
1575 I Street NW, Suite 400
Washington, D.C. 20005
aam-us.org
(202) 289-6578

Biocommunications

Biologists and other scientists communicate with each other using a language that is very technical and specific. It might as well be a foreign language to the rest of us. When a layperson or someone outside the discipline of biology must understand this information, there has to be a translator who can decipher the language of science. People who enter this field usually discover during their college years that they enjoy writing, talking about, or illustrating science more than doing experiments and participating in the actual research process. Many start by reporting on developments in biology or other science topics for their school newspapers or for a local newspaper or magazine. Writing promotional materials and newsletters for local museums and science centers is another way to gain experience in science journalism. All of these early assignments, even if only on a volunteer basis, help build a portfolio of published work that is important for that first real job in biocommunications. Supplementing science education with courses in journalism is also common.

Technical Writer

A technical writer translates a huge body of information into an easy-to-understand manual for a specific audience. Assignments usually involve writing instruction manuals or help files for computer software. The intended audience is usually other scientists, or it can also be anyone who is the client of the writer's employer. It sounds like a desk job for introverts, but most tech writers will tell you that you have to be a people person because you will need to get your information from the scientists who do the research, not from lab reports. Tech writers also have to be good team players because they often are assigned to groups of various types of professionals who develop, market, and sell products. To be a tech writer, you have to enjoy learning about new things and be attentive to details, while maintaining perspective on the level required by your readers and keeping an eye on the overall learning goals. It's a good job for people who can handle multiple projects at one time and are deadline-oriented.

A typical day includes meetings, checking e-mail, meeting with people to do research, and writing off and on all day. The hours are flexible, scheduled around meetings and deadlines. Some tech writers work at home or telecommute. For a writer, it is satisfying work because the end product is very helpful and more widely read than many scientific journal articles. Hazards of the job include repetitive stress injuries of the hands and wrists or eyestrain from using the computer. Some people also find that meeting deadlines can be stressful. The salary is generally between $45,000 and $50,000 per year. Freelance writers charge $50 to $60 an hour. Most experienced tech writers can make $70,000; more as managers or in-demand freelancers. Most tech writing jobs do not require a Ph.D., but an undergraduate degree in biology or another science is usually required. Also, some community colleges offer a certificate in technical writing.

Science Journalist

For scientists who like to write but are interested in reporting events to the general public, there is the career of science journalism. Even though a science journalist might have a degree in biology, he or she will probably have to report on the broader aspects of science. Science journalists work in a variety of settings, including the following:

- Universities, medical centers, research institutions have public information officers (PIO) who write for in-house publications and work on annual reports, press releases, and newsletters like the *Harvard Medical Letter.*
- Government research institutes like NIH and private biotech companies employ science journalists who serve as PIOs.
- Outside agencies are hired to write some or all of an institution's publications and press releases.
- Popular science magazines (*Discover, Science News, Popular Science*) and some general magazines (*Time, Newsweek*) have regular science columns.
- Publishers who produce biology textbooks and learning materials need science writers.
- Although it is often difficult to make a living at this, some freelance writers opt for self-employment.

As with technical writing, preparation for this career involves taking journalism courses. Other prerequisites include building a portfolio and enhancing your network of professional contacts by volunteering to write for local publications. This is an occupation that is expected to grow in the future. Salaries for science journalists working for newspapers and magazines range from $25,000 to $80,000. The larger the publication, the larger the salary. Moving up in this field often means moving to a larger publication, which may necessitate relocating. Starting salaries for public information officers can be $30,000 to $40,000. More experienced PIOs can make $60,000 or more. Freelancers are paid by the word on a scale of 25 cents to $2.00 per word. Openings can be found through the local newspaper or advertised on the Web page of the National Association of Science Writers; however, you'll probably get most of your jobs by networking with other professionals.

Science Illustrator

Biologists who want to pursue a career in art can become science illustrators. This is another field that does not require a Ph.D. but does require talent in drawing, photography, or other media. Some artists also work on 3-D models. Medical illustration is a specialized field dealing with the human body, or animals in veterinary medicine.

It is important to build a portfolio (samples of your work). You can start with samples of illustrations from reports and papers in school and should, definitely, include anything that you have had published. Science illustrators must be very knowledgeable about copyright laws both to protect their own work and to use the work of others. Universities with medical or veterinary schools or medical practices that do a lot of publishing and teaching employ science illustrators. About half are self-employed freelancers who work on contract for pharmaceutical companies, advertising companies, or publishers of books or journals. To be successful at freelancing you have to be a businessperson, and you should expect to spend up to half of your time on business-related activities. You need to be willing to market yourself and sometimes face rejection. However, the rewards are a good living and complete control over your own career path. The BioCommunications Association offers seminars and certification.

Broadcast Journalist

There has been a huge increase in the coverage of science in the media, including the advent of several cable television channels devoted to science. The Discovery Channel is one example. Almost all of the major television network news programs and many of the local affiliates have a very visible science broadcaster. Public radio and television were pioneers in the popularization of science. When you think of broadcast journalism, you probably associate it with the star of a show like Ira Flatow, the host of the National Public Radio (NPR) show "Science Friday," or Michael Guillen, Ph.D., who is the "Science Editor" for ABC's "Good Morning, America." Although these are the people we see or hear the most, there are many people behind the scenes whose knowledge of science is needed to produce these shows. If you are considering a career in broadcast journalism, there are a lot of jobs to choose from, but only one characteristic that you must bring to the job—a respect for deadlines. With or without you, the show must go on.

Reporters get assignments in two ways: from their editors or by finding their own material using wire services and reading newspapers and journal articles. They need to be able to sift through all of the scientific jargon and translate the newsworthy facts into short sound bites that the general public will understand and find fascinating.

The editor's job is to give assignments to the reporters and writers so that each show is written according to the producer's plan and is completed by its deadline. This requires juggling many programs at one time and always being ready to insert late-breaking news. Editors progress in the business by moving to bigger shows, so early in their careers they frequently are relocating. Networking with colleagues from previous jobs is how most editors find positions and promotions.

Broadcasters are the people we see in front of the camera or hear on the radio. In science, there are very few full-time broadcasters; NPR has the most. Most network broadcasters find themselves reporting not only on science news, but on health and technology news as well.

For more information, contact:

BioCommunications Association
220 Southwind Lane
Hillsborough, NC 27278
bca.org
(919) 245-0906

Canadian Science Writers' Association
40 Alexander Street, Suite 1111
Toronto, ON M4Y 1B5
Canada
(416) 928-9624
interlog.com/~cswa

Society for Technical Communication
901 North Stuart Street, Suite 904
Arlington, VA 22203
(703) 522-4114
stc.org

Society for Scholarly Publishing
10200 West Forty-Fourth Avenue, Suite 304
Wheat Ridge, CO 80033
(303) 422-3914
sspnet.org

Council of Biology Editors
60 Revere Drive, Suite 500
Northbrook, IL 60092
(847) 480-9080
http://cbe.org

National Association of Science Writers (NASW)
P.O. Box 294
Greenlawn, NY 11740
(516) 757-5664
nasw.org

Technology Transfer

People who work in the world of technology transfer deal with the commercialization of ideas that are discovered at public institutions, such as universities or government research labs. They manage all of the steps necessary to bring the ideas to the marketplace, including acquisitions, patenting and licensing, and publication of the new technology. Most of these positions are held by very senior administrators or executives who have the experience and expertise to recognize the cutting-edge ideas that have the potential to become practical applications of science. To succeed at this career, you need to be interested in the business of science and have good negotiating skills. In the university setting, you would contract with companies or venture capitalists to sponsor research at your institution, and you would handle the patenting, licensing, and marketing of technologies developed by your institution's researchers.

This is another field where a Ph.D. is not required; however, an advanced degree does command the respect of the Ph.D. researchers you deal with. Some tech transfer experts get an M.B.A. or law degree, depending on the focus of their jobs. Confidentiality is a major concern in this business.

The National Institutes of Health sponsors seminars on technology transfer for those who are interested in knowing more about the field. The demand for experts in technology transfer has dramatically increased as government research funding is reduced. Universities and other research institutions are becoming more dependent on tech transfer liaisons who can find business partners in the private sector to fund the basic science work that is so important to all of us. In 1980 the Bayh-Dole Act was passed. It allowed scientists to collect royalties on any government-funded research that was commercialized. Many universities started their own technology transfer departments to explore the income possibilities of their research operations, and they employ many scientists who are interested in making a transition from the lab to business. Starting salaries range from $40,000 to $60,000 for entry-level university jobs.

For more information, contact:

Association of University Technology Managers (AUTM)
49 East Avenue
Norwalk, CT 06851
(203) 845-9015
autm.net

Sales and Marketing

Sales and marketing requires good people skills and an interest in the products and services that are purchased by research industry buyers. Although many successful salespeople in the science marketplace are not scientists, having a science background can give you an edge when your customers are also scientists. A scientist's technical background as well as his or her communications skills and ability to solve problems quickly are often an advantage in this job. It is also a field where entry-level positions abound. If you can sell ten to twenty times what you are paid, the industry considers you a good investment.

There are sales techniques that need to be learned, but other characteristics such as respecting deadlines and budgets and adhering to strict quality guidelines— in this setting, for customer service—give science-trained salespeople the edge. Unlike the laboratory, sales jobs generally require a lot of travel and can be stressful when you are faced with quotas that must be met by a particular deadline. In addition, you must learn to deal with the financial ups and downs of not collecting a regular paycheck. Salespeople get paid in a lot of different ways. If you are successful, the lack of a regular paycheck is not important if you are periodically collecting large commissions and getting bonuses and perquisites like a company car or frequent flyer miles that can be used for a free vacation.

Scientists who want to become salespeople often start as the technical support person for a sales department, or they work on the customer help desk as technical support. This is an important transition because many successful salespeople market themselves as resource persons to their clients.

Law

Scientists who work in the law generally specialize in intellectual property or the legal protection of ideas, research, theories, and so forth. The American Bar Association further defines this specialty as: patents, trademarks, copyrights, and trade secrets. Scientists-turned-lawyers also work in the areas of medical device product liability and environmental law. Insiders say that this is one career where a Ph.D. may not be an asset. There are many more law school graduates and the field is very competitive. Law firms may see hiring a science expert as too expensive an option, and having technical knowledge is sometimes not an advantage over experience as a lawyer.

Biolegal work is available in a variety of settings including staff counsel in corporations, universities, law firms, or government agencies. Some scientists who are interested in patent law often take the patent bar examination offered by the U.S. Patent Office before completing law school. They can work for a patent examiner prior to finishing their law degree. This is another career where it is good to do some informational interviewing to find out about its unique characteristics, such as travel and night school options.

For more information, contact:

American Bar Association
(Section on Intellectual Property and Section on Science
    and Technology)
750 North Lake Shore Drive
Chicago, IL 60611
(312) 988-5000
abanet.org

Environmental Law Institute
1616 P Street NW, Suite 200
Washington, D.C. 20036
(202) 939-3639
eli.org

Council of Canadian Law Deans
57 Louis-Pasteur
Ottawa, ON K1N 6N5
Canada
canadalawschools.org

Science Policy and Advocacy

This is a career choice that requires that you have an interest in politics and one in which you find the machinations of government fascinating, not frustrating. Since most scientists have difficulty communicating with Congress and government agencies, they hire advocates who can convey the perspective of the scientific community to laypersons in the government. This requires not only excellent communications skills, but also the ability to network with the right people, a talent for negotiation, effective conflict resolution skills, and the belief that you can be an agent of change. If you regularly read the policy sections of science societies' publications and websites and avidly follow political news on science issues, this might be your niche.

You might try giving this career a test run by writing about science for a general-interest publication or by volunteering at the office of a local politician, including getting involved in campaigns or working on science-related issues for your candidate. There are also several internship programs, including the Congressional Science Fellows program Research! America, which sponsors six types of policy fellowships.

For more information, contact:

American Association for the Advancement of Science (AAAS)
Fellowship Programs
1200 New York Avenue NW
Washington, D.C. 20005
(202) 326-6600
aaas.org

Regulatory Affairs

The two areas of complex government regulations in the biological sciences are in the health sciences, including pharmaceuticals and the environment. People who choose to enter the regulatory arena have to know how to negotiate the legally required steps to bring a product to market from the research bench or to offer a product to consumers without compromising the environment. Most professionals in this field work in biotechnology and pharmaceuticals, but others are experts on regulations concerning veterinary, cosmetics, in vitro testing, and food sciences. On the environmental side, mastery of the myriad EPA regulations is a necessity.

To be successful in regulatory affairs, you must be very detail-oriented, since an important part of this job is the responsibility for scrutinizing documents that must be submitted to government agencies. Errors in this documentation can cause costly delays. The duties of the regulatory affairs officer can sometimes include quality assurance (QA), and for this reason, it is sometimes easier to start in QA and transition to a job in regulatory affairs. Another strategy is to move into an entry-level job in the regulatory affairs department of the company where you work. It is very hard to find a first job if you are inexperienced and do not have an inside track.

Once established, you will find that there are a lot of choices for experienced people. It is one of those careers that is difficult to get a start in; there are no volunteer opportunities because of the trade secrets that are at risk. If you have any experience with any type of regulations in your current job, you might want to emphasize it. Also, there is certification available from the Regulatory Affairs Personnel Society. There are a few universities that offer an advanced degree in this field.

For more information, contact:

Regulatory Affairs Professionals Society (RAPS)
12300 Twinbrook Parkway, Suite 350
Rockville, MD 20852
(301) 770-2920
raps.org

Forensic Biology

Forensic biologists provide the scientific analysis of biological evidence, such as blood, semen, or saliva, that is related to a crime. DNA, everyone's unique genetic signature, is used to identify suspects, crime scenes, or weapons used in a crime and to re-create the sequence of events. Much of this analysis is performed in a laboratory using technology such as a "Luma Lite," which helps to locate evidence that is not visible to the naked eye. Some forensic specialists also go to the scene to collect evidence. In situations where a forensic scientist is on call, there is usually compensation in the form of extra pay or time off.

In addition to good technical skills, forensic scientists must also be good at speaking in public, as they are sometimes asked to testify in court and must be able to write a scientific report. These communications skills include the ability to translate, in a very objective way, the scientific findings of the laboratory investigation into information that can be understood by the nonscientists involved in the case. Excellent computer skills are a must and intellectual curiosity keeps the job interesting. Generally, the work schedule involves regular business hours, and universities, large police departments, private companies, or agencies of the local, state, or federal governments, including the FBI, run the laboratories.

There are various levels of employment starting with forensic lab technician, a position that requires an associate's (two-year) degree in forensics. Starting salaries for entry-level jobs tend to be around $20,000 per year. A bachelor's degree in biology with some training in forensics is the best preparation for this type of career, and it gives you flexibility for future growth or a career change. Salaries start at around $30,000 and can go up to about $60,000. Some scientists go for further training in other subspecialties of forensic biology, including entomology, zoology, or botany.

There are also several careers in forensics for medical doctors who are interested in this field. A forensic pathologist, sometimes called a medical examiner in larger cities and municipalities, is a medical doctor who specializes in examining unexplained deaths by doing autopsies, which are exploratory operations on the deceased. Using the results of the autopsy and other information such as medical records, a forensic pathologist must determine the cause of death and sometimes can reconstruct the circumstances of the death. The pathologist's findings are usually included in the court proceeding if a crime has been committed, and the pathologist is often called to testify as an expert witness in the case. This career requires a medical degree as well as a residency and fellowship in the specialty.

In most medical examiners' departments, there are also autopsy assistants who assist the physician with his or her work. Their training and opportunities are similar to those of the forensic lab technician. Other forensic medical specialties include forensic psychiatrists, who deal with the behavioral aspects of a crime such as competency to stand trial, state of mental functioning at the time of a commission of a crime, and profiling of criminals. For those who have chosen to pursue a doctorate in dentistry, there is also forensic odontology, or forensic dentistry. These professionals are key in the identification of victims of crimes where teeth and dental work are the only remains or where a bite mark would identify a criminal. Whatever the level of employment, careers in forensic biology are expected to grow significantly, as the demand for scientific evidence increases.

For more information, contact:

American Academy of Forensic Science (AAFS)
P.O. Box 669
410 North Twenty-First Street
Colorado Springs, CO 80904-2798
(719) 636-1100
aafs.org (click on Resources menu; select "Choosing a Career")

Biosciences Librarians and Information Service Providers

An information explosion has taken place in the world. Use of the Internet has made access to almost any kind of information possible from your home computer. Without people to organize this mass of facts and make it accessible to us, it would be useless. Those people are librarians and information specialists. In the biosciences, a librarian would have to have a background, possibly a bachelor's degree, in biology or the life sciences and a master's degree in library and information science. There is also a specialty in library science for health sciences librarians who work in hospitals, medical schools, and medical research facilities. Many health sciences librarians are also employed in the pharmaceutical industry. Generally, librarians are responsible for organizing and disseminating information from a library facility that might house books, journals or magazines, audiovisual materials, or computer disks and CD-ROMs.

These days, the science librarian is also very likely to be managing in-house databases as well as Internet access to proprietary databases that provide very specialized—and often very expensive—information to researchers. On the opposite side of the technology spectrum are corporate or institution archives or historical records. The responsibility for the maintenance of these materials often falls to the librarian. It is a very diverse job that requires a curiosity about all aspects of the biosciences and tremendous organizational skills that must keep up with advances in technology.

Special librarians like those who work in the biosciences are among the highest-paid workers in the profession. Some biosciences librarians work for proprietary (entrepreneurial) database developers and vendors who gather, organize, and disseminate very specialized information to clients—often science libraries. This information may come from other scientists or it may be about the industry. It is usually very current and not available through other sources such as printed media. Sometimes the services abstract the masses of information that are available through printed materials like journals, press releases, newspaper articles, and so forth. It is difficult for scientists to read everything in their field. These information companies usually provide computerized retrieval services online, very much like using an Internet search engine. An information specialist who works for a data service such as this would be responsible for identifying information to be added to the database, categorizing it for easy retrieval, and possibly designing new ways for clients to interface with the database that ensure easy use.

For more information, contact:

Special Libraries Association (SLA)
1700 Eighteenth Street NW
Washington, D.C. 20009-4700
(202) 234-4700
sla.org

Clinical Research

Clinical research differs from laboratory research because of where it takes place—not in the laboratory, but at the site of clinical trials research. Clinical trials are the testing procedures that the Federal Drug Administration (FDA) requires before a drug or biomedical device can be marketed to the public. Since these trials usually involve testing a new product on human beings, a significant number of laboratory studies precede the human studies to ensure that they are safe. The FDA has very strict protocols or procedures that must be followed, so that the human subjects are tested safely and the information that is gathered about both the good and bad effects of the new drug or device can be evaluated impartially.

In a clinical trial, there is a group of people who do the hands-on testing. Such a group includes a chief investigator, who is in charge of the protocol, and several other people, usually nurses, who are specially trained in clinical research and actually recruit and meet with patients, perform the trial procedures, and gather the data that will be analyzed and put into the FDA documentation. There is typically another group of people, clinical research professionals, who work for the agency that is responsible for overseeing the trials. These professionals can have various backgrounds, but they are usually trained in the biosciences or biomedical sciences and have educational degrees varying from the bachelor's to the Ph.D. Their job involves developing the clinical protocols according to FDA guidelines, finding hospitals or medical clinics where the new products can be tested, monitoring the testing sites to make sure that they are in compliance with the protocol, collecting and analyzing the data from the sites, and preparing the documentation for the FDA. A pharmaceutical or biotechnology company, a large university research center, or, more recently, private companies that specialize in this work and contract out to clients who do the hands-on testing employ clinical research associates.

There are currently about seventeen thousand active members of the Association of Clinical Research Professionals (ACRP), ten thousand of which are certified in one of three categories: clinical research coordinator (on-site researcher), clinical research associate (monitoring functions), and clinical research investigator (M.D. or Ph.D. chief investigator). Preparation for the certification exam and continuing education is available from the ACRP, as are job opportunities. In addition to research lab work, some experience with patients in a clinical setting is a plus in entering this field.

For more information, contact:

Association of Clinical Research Professionals
5000 Montgomery Street, Suite 800
Alexandria, VA 22314
(703) 254-8100
acrpnet.org

8

PREPARING FOR YOUR CAREER IN THE BIOLOGICAL SCIENCES

THE EDUCATION OF a biologist requires a large investment of time and money. So before you commit yourself, why not take a test ride? Fortunately there are several ways to test your perception of what your job choice would be like against the reality of how you feel when you actually are working in that environment with people who could be your coworkers.

Volunteer or part-time work and internships are an excellent way to try out a career by actually doing it. In addition, using a personal computer to log onto Internet websites to communicate with real scientists and scientific organizations is helpful in finding out what life is like on the job. A combination of real and virtual time spent visualizing yourself as a biologist is a smart way of trying on a career before finding out, in the senior year of an undergraduate program, that it's not for you.

How do you find a job once you have finished your volunteer and virtual rehearsal and completed your educational road map?

The last part of this chapter offers some suggestions for strategies that work.

Trying a Career in Biology on for Size

Volunteerism is in! Many people are finding that giving to other people and organizations enriches their lives in ways that paychecks can't. First think about where you would like to work. Without a Ph.D. you may not be able to do the job you would like to have someday, but if you can get your foot in the door as a volunteer, you would have a chance to mingle with scientists who are what you want to become. Also, if you have never worked in this type of environment, it would give you some experience in acclimating to the work schedule and other aspects of the organizational culture. You may have to start at the bottom of the career ladder—type and file paperwork, clean cages, answer the phone, give tours to visitors, straighten the lab, and so forth. But it's a chance to keep your eyes and ears open and to ask questions to your heart's content.

You can find places to work in a number of ways:

- Look in the Yellow Pages of the phone book.
- Contact some of the associations listed in each chapter of this book to ask for a list of members or sites that might have volunteer opportunities.
- Go to your local public library and ask the librarian to help you find a list of volunteer organizations or a Chamber of Commerce directory in your area that would list the type of organization you are interested in.
- Ask your biology teacher and guidance counselor.

Part-time jobs are becoming more plentiful and better paid. The first place to look might be the employment section of the newspaper or the job bulletin board at school. You also might try the same sources listed above for volunteer opportunities, but call to ask for part-time work instead. One of the best strategies for job hunting, part-time or full-time, is networking. Tell everyone you know that you want to find a part-time job that will help you try your intended career in biology on for size. You might be surprised to know someone who knows a biologist who needs a part-time helper.

Prepare a short one-page résumé that outlines your qualifications for the job. Include things such as volunteer work, sports, committee work, offices held, and courses taken at school. Take a job in the company or organization that employs the type of professional you wish to become and then find that someone. Ask that person to be your mentor, someone who will give you the personal and professional advice to become the type of biologist you want to become.

Internships are generally educational experiences that are designed to give the participant exposure to a future career. Summer internships are becoming more popular with nonprofit organizations that need help but have limited funding. For you, an internship is an excellent opportunity to try a career, because instead of pay, you can structure an educational experience that might expose you to more experiences than would a part-time or volunteer job. Many organizations use interns to help with special projects that they do not have staff or time to accomplish. As part of the educational experience, you will probably be required to write a paper, do a presentation, or complete an assigned project.

Your high school or college also may grant academic credit for your internship, if it is approved ahead of time. You can locate internships by contacting the professional organizations listed in this book or by calling an organization where you would like to work. If the organization does not have an internship program, ask to meet with a staff member who needs help with a special project and submit a proposal for an educational experience that would help both you and your mentor. Who could resist a go-getter intern like that?

Don't forget to keep a record of exactly what you do as a volunteer or part-timer. This experience will form the basis of a résumé that you can use for later jobs. It will show your early commitment to your chosen career. Make sure that you keep up-to-date information about the people who can provide references for you.

The Virtual Biologist

Throughout this book there are references to the Internet or to websites on it. If you are not computer literate or have never used the Internet, it is time to explore this exciting resource. You can get the training you need at school or check with your local library. Larger public libraries frequently have computers where you can learn about and use the Net.

Once you know how to access the Web, you will find that typing "biology careers" into your search software will connect you with some of the most interesting sites that contain pages of information, including color photographs. This information can be downloaded into your personal computer and then printed. In addition, you can interact with researchers on the cutting edge of the biological sciences or other disciplines by logging onto a website like Scientific American. You can ask questions or read their responses to others.

Other ways of experiencing the world of the biologist before you take the plunge is to read what they read. You can use the Internet to peruse the full text of many scientific periodicals and documents without traveling to a university library. Almost every college and university has its biology department's curricula and information about student life available on its Web page. You also can review the credentials and interests of faculty members who might become your role models. Sometimes it is possible to access students' homework assignments or review their reading materials to get an idea of the scope and difficulty of a particular course.

Posting your résumé online is a popular way to job hunt. You can compare your experience and plans with those of young biologists who are upwardly mobile.

Navigating Your Educational Road Map

The educational road map for biologists is like that of many other professionals. It includes a high school program with a concentration in the life and physical sciences. It also includes as broad a selection of subjects as possible, including English, mathematics, computer science, social studies, and extracurricular activities that show that a future scientist has a well-balanced character as well as academic achievement. College courses at the undergraduate level, leading to a Bachelor of Science degree in the biological sciences, should provide a broad training program in the first years followed by a concentration on the major subject. Then, after graduation, a more intense concentration will follow on a narrower aspect of the major through the acquisition of a master's degree and finally a doctorate. Most graduate biologists also pursue several years of postdoctoral training, where they become apprentice scientists somewhat comparable to the internship and residency requirements of a medical specialist. Many graduate students and "post docs" teach as well as learn in the final years of their formal education. All these steps are important for those who will fill the highest positions as research scientists or university professors.

If you are considering a career in biology, the level of education you pursue beyond high school depends upon what place you wish eventually to assume on the biological team. If you wish to work in a laboratory, there are schools that take high school graduates and train them in a couple of years to be laboratory technicians. Their graduates have no trouble obtaining jobs with good pay. They work in doctors' offices, hospital laboratories, or various research centers. For advancement, however, further education must be obtained. For one of the best jobs as a laboratory technician, you will need to finish college.

Your educational plan does not have to include continuous education. It is not unusual for a young high school or college graduate to accept a job as laboratory assistant or technician with the intention of continuing study as time permits, earning credits toward a degree. Some have gone all the way through college and on to the Ph.D. degree this way. It may be done by part-time schooling or by alternately working and studying full-time. Some employers, especially industrial laboratories and some government departments, encourage employees to improve their education by permitting time off for class attendance and by paying tuition bills.

It has been said that the scientist speaks with three kinds of languages: English, mathematics, and foreign languages. High school is not too soon to start the mastery of all three. English is the language you will be using to communicate with your fellow students and with your fellow scientists; you should strive to speak and write it correctly, concisely, and with the precise meaning you wish to convey. The use of mathematics varies greatly among the various fields of biology, but more and more biologists need to know at least calculus and statistics. For some of the newer fields of research, such as molecular biology and biophysics, more advanced mathematics is required. Because science knows no international boundaries, much information that's important to biologists—especially if they are engaged in research—is published in languages other than English. At international gatherings of bioscientists, it is necessary to communicate with people who speak other languages. For these reasons, certain language requirements have been established for students majoring in biology or other sciences. The high school student intending to go on through graduate school should anticipate these requirements and start language study as early as possible. If language study were postponed, it would require time that those advanced students would prefer to devote to their specialty.

Today's high school curriculum teaches all students to be more "bioliterate" whether they choose the life sciences as a career or not. Biology today is about how humans interact with their living environment. Students are engaged in the exploration of the ecology of their environment and in their own health and wellness. They learn what it means to be a part of a biodiverse universe, which is a lot more interesting than training as a lab assistant. In addition to English, mathematics, and language, high school students interested in any science should include chemistry, physics, computer science, and advanced courses in biology in their programs. Most high schools offer computer science. Good skills in the use of the personal computer will be helpful in college and in your career. Many computer users find a typing course to be an invaluable prerequisite to efficient computing. With these studies, together with the basic requirements for graduation, the student will enter college well prepared to pursue any course of study—biology, another science, or nonscience.

Undergraduate education for the biosciences in currently undergoing a dramatic change. Many experts in the field believe that most colleges and universities have not kept up with the revolutionary way that biological research is conducted today. In an effort to encourage institutions to make a quicker change in undergraduate biology education, the National Research Council (NRC) assembled a team of experts who were charged with developing strategies and curricula for the "new biology" to be taught in colleges and universities. Their report is entitled "BIO2010: Transforming Undergraduate Education for Future Research Biologists." It is a very long report, but anyone who is thinking of enrolling in an undergraduate biology program should read the "Executive Summary" and be familiar with the main points. Then, as part of your college selection process, compare the undergraduate programs of prospective colleges with the NRC recommendations.

The report can be viewed on the NRC's website. Here are some of the major recommendations contained in it:

- Students will need more scientific knowledge, practice with scientific design, quantitative abilities, and communications skills.
- Science and math courses should emphasize the process of discovery, not just the memorization of facts.
- Laboratory work should provide students with the opportunity to experience research in a real-world environment; class projects would simulate the research environment through experiences such as analysis of original data, teamwork, computer modeling, scientific writing, and presentation.

- Besides biology courses, students need to be well educated in mathematics, bioinformatics, and the physical sciences (physics, chemistry).
- Colleges should offer seminar-type courses that encourage collaborative relationships between students and faculty/mentors, emphasize the cutting edge of biological research, and attract students to a career in biological research.
- Efforts should be made to find time and money for biology faculty to "retool" curricula and themselves for this new approach to education.

In addition to these recommendations, the NRC report acknowledges that many undergraduate programs have focused on preparing their biology majors who are premed students for the Medical College Admissions Test (MCAT). This test has not kept pace with changes in the world of biology, and it competes with rather than complements the needed reforms in biosciences education. The NRC recommends, therefore, that the test be revised to reflect the skills needed by premeds today and in the future. For more information on BIO2010, go to nap.edu and type BIO2010 in the title search section.

In many foreign countries, there is no exact equivalent to the baccalaureate or master's degrees, but the doctor of philosophy is universally recognized and respected as the highest official reward for the completion of a course of study aimed at the training of scholars, teachers, and research workers. There are some variations in the requirements from one university to another, but essentially they all include completion of certain prescribed courses; fulfilling requirements for a reading knowledge of one or more foreign languages of material in the candidate's major (this requirement has varied more in recent years than have the others); writing a dissertation (thesis) that presents and discusses the results of the student's original research; and passing special examinations, usually consisting of written examinations testing the student's broad knowledge of the subject and a final oral examination centering upon the points covered by the thesis.

The degree of doctor of philosophy (Ph.D.) has a venerable history and may be rewarded in many fields having no relation to science. Some universities, wishing to emphasize the concentration on science, award the degree of doctor of science (D.Sc.) rather than the Ph.D., just as in some instances the baccalaureate degree is B.S. instead of B.A. In each case, the degrees are equivalent.

In most institutions of higher learning, promotion and salary increases are based upon research success and especially upon scholarly publication. Often teaching ability is scarcely considered, and tenure may be denied to excellent teachers who have been less than prolific in publication—a situation known among college faculty members as "publish or perish."

Meeting Educational Costs

The cost of an education in biology at the undergraduate level does not differ from the cost of any other college education at the same level. Those who elect to continue their education in graduate school usually will find no difficulty in achieving an earning-while-learning status.

It is difficult to generalize on the costs of a college education; the costs vary greatly among different colleges and universities, and in the past several years they seem to have increased each year. High school students should not wait until near their graduation to decide what kind of college they want to attend, to take stock of their financial resources, and to examine the possibilities available in scholarships and loans to help defray expenses. Students should make full use of the information and help available from their high school guidance counselor and from other sources.

When the high school graduate applies for college entrance, he or she will find plenty of competition, even if the applicant has a good high school record and a high SAT score. There are some colleges that accept only the highest-ranking high school graduates, and some of the prestigious colleges have many times as many applicants as they can admit. For this reason, some students get an exaggerated idea of the difficulties in being accepted in college. Some of the lesser-known colleges may start the school year with vacancies in the freshman class. Some of these can offer a highly rewarding four years of college, with good training in selected fields—some of them in biological sciences—at costs appreciably lower than those of the big-name schools.

The student with a minimal budget may attend an excellent community college. Tuition is usually lower and most are located within commuting distance of home, which may eliminate the expense of room and board. The American Institute of Biological Sciences (AIBS) has been especially helpful in promoting professional activities by bioscientists in two-year colleges, and many of these schools have developed programs in general biology comparable to (and sometimes better than) those in the lower divisions of some four-year colleges.

State colleges offer a college education at a cost that is often several thousand dollars a year less than that prevailing at a private college of comparable eminence. In recent years, college tuition generally increased faster than the nation's inflation rate; college administrators blamed this situation on several factors, including the necessity to bring faculty salaries within the limits of other professions and to repair buildings that had long been neglected. However, the student faced with the necessity of meeting these costs will find that the colleges have also increased financial aid to qualifying students. This often enables a student with limited financial resources to attend a more expensive school. The selection of recipients of scholarships and loans is usually based on need as well as on past achievements, so most of the funds are reserved for those who need them most. Guidance counselors generally have much information on financial aid and the qualifications for applying, but it may also be helpful for the student to do some independent investigation.

There are many books and websites with information on scholarships, fellowships, and loans. For a more personalized approach to finding the right type of financial aid, make an appointment with your school's guidance or career counselor. He or she is often aware of special work-study programs, awards, and prizes that are not published in larger directories and may be offered only in your geographical area or might fit your particular circumstances. Financial aid counselors might have information, for instance, about special grants for certain ethnic groups, or for members of a fraternal organization or labor union, or for former military personnel.

Biology students are particularly fortunate in the number of part-time jobs available to them. In addition to the usual types of jobs that any college student may fill, some colleges employ students as part-time laboratory assistants. In some instances, the advanced biology student may even help out in the laboratory teaching of elementary courses. This provides valuable experience as well as a modest amount of financial aid. The young biologist may even be lucky enough to find employment in a particular branch of biology that will turn out to be a major interest in life.

Strange as it may seem, the financing of the graduate education leading to the doctoral degree is usually easier and simpler than that of the undergraduate years. Universities are eager to get talented graduate students for appointment as teaching assistants—or teaching fellows, as they are often called. In return for their help in teaching laboratory work in beginning biology courses, teaching fellows receive cash stipends and often free tuition for their graduate studies. In the larger universities with numerous graduate students, so much of the teaching is done by teaching fellows that these universities are often criticized for lack of contact between the undergraduate student and the eminent professors who are listed in the university catalog as teachers.

Biological research at universities is often financed by grants from governmental agencies, private foundations, or industrial firms. A large share of these funds is used for fellowships and research assistantships for students. Although some of these funds may be available for undergraduates, they are primarily for graduate study. Information on these sources is listed in the *Annual Register of Grant Support*, published by Marquis Professional Publications. It is good to know that it may be available when you need it, if your college record is good.

Finding That Job

One of the most popular ways to hunt for jobs today is by using the Internet. A good example of a very useful website is Science's Next Wave (nextwave.org), which is sponsored by the American Association for the Advancement of Science (AAAS). Access to many of the services offered at this website are free, like links to the classified ads in major publications and from some scientific associations. Other services such as salary surveys and reports on hiring trends require becoming a member of AAAS or paying a small monthly fee for access to the website.

For first-time job hunters or career changers, informational interviewing is an effective technique for learning about your intended career and, at the same time, building a network of contacts. Informational interviews are used to gain knowledge about a career choice by meeting with an expert who is already working in that field. The intent is not to get a job offer from that person, but to gain an insider's perspective on whether the job is a good fit for you, and if so, how to approach your job quest. You should go to the interview well prepared to ask intelligent questions; take your résumé for feedback on whether you are qualified for work in this field. Informational interviews rarely result in job offers, but frequently, if you do your homework and make a good impression, your interviewee will give your résumé to someone who might hire you. That's how networking begins.

Many colleges have placement bureaus that assist their students and graduates in finding jobs. Companies often send recruiters to campuses for employment interviews. Although many of these recruiters are looking for graduate students about to complete their requirements for a doctorate, openings at a lower level also are sometimes available in these interviews.

Many professional, scientific, and trade journals have classified sections with advertisements for "Positions Wanted" and "Positions Open." Among these are prestigious scientific journals such as *Science, Nature, BioScience, Genetics*, and *Federation Proceedings, Federation of American Societies for Experimental Biology*. Others are special trade periodicals; among those in this category that announce jobs of biological interest are *American Fruit Grower, American Vegetable Grower and Greenhouse Grower, The Commercial Fisheries News, Pulp & Paper, Wines and Vines*, and many others. Then there are those of regional interest, or those aiming their appeal to special groups, such as *California Farmer, Pacific Coast Nurseryman and Garden Supply Dealer, Southern Florist and Nurseryman, The Black Collegian Magazine*, and *Black Careers*.

Besides these opportunities for full-time jobs, there are often opportunities for young graduates to obtain graduate fellowships; these are frequently advertised in scientific journals. Not to be overlooked are the "Help Wanted" columns of major city newspapers. Some of these, such as the *New York Times, Washington Post,* and *Chicago Tribune*, carry ads of more than local interest in their particular geographic area. Advertised in this way, jobs can draw many hundreds of responses, and this reduces the chances of any one applicant. It is clear, then, that in looking for a job one should not rely exclusively on such ads, but if you use them, they should be answered promptly, and you should scan the paper not just once, but with perseverance.

Scientific societies take an interest in helping employers and prospective employees get together. This interest may be implemented in one or more of several different ways: by advertisements in the official journal or website of the society, by maintaining placement services in the society's office, or by arranging job interviews at the annual meeting of the organization.

Each specialty in bioscience boasts its own society—such organizations as the American Association of Anatomists, American Society for Microbiology, and Botanical Society of America. The societies also band together both on a national and an international scale. The qualifications for membership in these societies vary widely. In some cases, it is only necessary to express an interest in the society and pay the dues; others admit to membership only those who have demonstrated ability to conduct and publish results of research in a particular field. Some have more than one category of membership, welcoming not only established professionals but also beginners, with special provision for students.

Science transcends international boundaries, so many of the national societies belong to International Unions, and these in turn make up one grand overall organization called the International Council of Scientific Unions (ICSU). The council's function is to promote meetings in which scientists of various nations get together and exchange information on their latest research findings. On a national scale, the American Association for the Advancement of Science (AAAS) includes scientists of all disciplines, including bioscience. In many states or other local areas there is also a local Academy of Science. The AAAS is an association of many scientific societies, both physical and life sciences, but the individual scientist is also a member of the AAAS, and indeed nonscientists or those not members of any constituent society also are welcomed as members. Annual meetings of the AAAS give beginners an opportunity to meet established scientists and obtain job interviews.

Associations of biological societies of special interest to biologists are the American Institute of Biological Sciences (AIBS) and the Federation of American Societies for Experimental Biology (FASEB). These two large associations are supplemented by societies that belong to no federation. FASEB is primarily of interest to those engaged in research in a biomedical science, as will become apparent by the following constituent societies: American Physiological Society, American Society for Biochemistry and Molecular

Biology, American Society for Pharmacology and Experimental Therapeutics, American Association of Pathologists, American Institute of Nutrition, American Association of Immunologists, and American Society for Cell Biology. FASEB does not accept individuals as members, but one is a member of FASEB only by virtue of membership in one or more of the constituent societies. However, nonmembers, especially students, are welcome at meetings, they may present papers, and—most importantly for our present discussion—FASEB operates a placement service that maintains a list of employers with vacancies and those looking for jobs. The list is published annually. In addition, interviews are scheduled between employers and prospective employees.

The largest organization of biologists is AIBS. It is a federation of biological societies, but unlike FASEB, it also accepts individual members. AIBS merits the support of all biologists, and indeed its goal is to enroll all professional biologists. AIBS has provided consulting services for many governmental agencies and private foundations; it has served groups such as the Environmental Protection Agency, the National Science Foundation, and the Food and Drug Administration. AIBS keeps up-to-date records of biographical and professional information concerning bioscientists, and it publishes periodicals that keep members and subscribers informed on current interests of biology and biological education.

The Education Committee of AIBS is of special importance to students and teachers or to anyone contemplating a biological career. This committee is actively engaged in career guidance and handles many thousands of requests for career information. These requests come from students, faculty, guidance counselors, and others. The office has sponsored and guided bioscience curriculum studies that have largely revolutionized the teaching of biology in high schools and colleges. Its activities include the preparation and updating of a free brochure, *Careers in Biology*, as well as aiding in the dissemination of career booklets prepared by the individual societies that make up AIBS. AIBS also charters student chapters in high schools and colleges throughout the country. Participation in a student chapter provides an opportunity for students to maintain contact with biologists and biology professionals all over the country and to gain insight into what biology as a profession is all about.

AIBS maintains a placement service that supplies lists to candidates and to employers so that they can meet by correspondence or for personal interviews at the annual convention. Each year, many biologists, especially beginners, get to meet prospective employers this way. Either FASEB or AIBS will be glad to answer any questions regarding careers or employment at these addresses:

FASEB Placement Service
9650 Rockville Pike
Bethesda, MD 20814

AIBS Education Committee
730 Eleventh Street NW
Washington, D.C. 20001

As you can see, there are many different ways for a biologist to look for a job. Perhaps the most important of all is networking through personal contacts. This is especially true as one advances in the profession. During the early stages of a biologist's career, as the student is about to graduate from college, the professors with whom one has been studying will have received notices of fellowships, graduate assistantships, and various teaching, service, or research jobs available to graduates. In many departments, such notices are regularly posted on the bulletin boards; there also will be some on the professor's desks. Some of these vacancies will be available to those just completing study for a baccalaureate degree; others will be for those about to receive the doctorate. Either way, there is a good chance that one's professor is personally acquainted with the prospective employer. In that case, it is more than likely that the personal recommendation of the professor will carry more weight with the employer than any other single document or record the candidate can produce.

About the Author

KATHLEEN BELIKOFF PERSONIFIES the idea that career opportunities abound for people who are willing to work their way up. Her own career in health care began when she took a temporary job as a medical records file clerk. She became a hospital administrator at Presbyterian Medical Center in Philadelphia and is now a health care consultant.

Ms. Belikoff grew up in suburban Baltimore and began her writing career as editor-in-chief of the Hereford High School student newspaper. She honed her writing skills as an English major at Hood College and pursued a graduate degree in education and information science at Towson State University. Her most recent publications are about her observations on the changing health care scene, including a chapter in *Using Hospital Space Profitably* about converting unused hospital space into restaurants, research labs, and other revenue-producing facilities.

Her interest in writing about eye care career opportunities emanates from her association with the world-renowned Scheie Eye

Institute, which serves as the department of ophthalmology for both Presbyterian and the University of Pennsylvania hospitals. Starting as the hospital librarian and later as an administrator, she worked with all levels of clinical staff, researchers, administrators, medical and nursing students, and patients. Today, she continues to write about health careers and works with graduate students in nursing, computer science, business, and education as a reference librarian at the Bucks County Campus of La Salle University.